GRANDMA TODAY

Traditional Treats for Busy Cooks

Dee' 94

Dear Deirdre,

Happy Cooking!
Verna & Irene

by Irene Hrechuk
& Verna Zasada

**Front Cover: Spinach Waldorf Salad with Poppy Seed
Dressing, page 75
Lemon Yogurt Scones, page 19**

GRANDMA TODAY
by
Irene Hrechuk & Verna Zasada

First Printing — September 1994

Copyright © 1994 by
Averine Enterprises Ltd.
116 Langholm Drive
St. Albert, Alberta
Canada   T8N 4M4

Canadian Cataloguing in Publication Data

Hrechuk, Irene, 1943 —

Grandma today

Includes index.
ISBN 1-895292-42-5

1. Cookery.   I. Zasada, Verna, 1934 —   I. Title.

TX725.A1H73 1994   641.5   C94-920234-7

Food Photography by
Merle Prosofsky
Merle Prosofsky Photography
Edmonton, Alberta

Authors' Portrait by
Ron McDonald
Edmonton, Alberta

Dishes and Accessories Compliments of
Bosch Kitchen Centre, Edmonton
Eaton's

Designed, Printed and Produced in Canada by:
Centax Books, a Division of PrintWest Communications Ltd.
Publishing Director, Photo Designer & Food Stylist: Margo Embury
1150 Eighth Avenue, Regina, Saskatchewan, Canada S4R 1C9
(306) 525-2304   FAX: (306) 757-2439

TABLE OF CONTENTS

Recipes have been tested in U.S. Standard measurements. Common metric measurements are given as a convenience for those who are more familiar with metric. Recipes have not been tested in metric.

INTRODUCTION

Grandma's cooking will always evoke warm memories of tantalizing aromas and flavors. Grandma's role has changed over the years. Today she often has a hectic schedule as she carries out her career goals while being an integral part of the lives of her children and grandchildren. This change in lifestyle has made scratch cooking a less common event in her kitchen.

The recipes in *Grandma Today* reflect a move toward easier food preparation while retaining the down-to-earth goodness we associate with grandma's cooking. With an emphasis on healthier eating due to our changing lifestyle, many of these recipes are adapted to using ingredients with less fat or sodium or allow for substitutions. With our access to a wide variety of international ingredients, grandma's cooking reflects a more cosmopolitan use of spices, herbs and other ingredients. This allows for greater flexibility in preparing, serving and experimenting to find flavor and texture combinations which appeal to family and friends.

We trust that you will enjoy this collection. We have retained the simplicity and satisfying flavors that you enjoyed in *Grandma's Touch* while introducing some convenience ingredients to allow for quick preparation as part of your busy schedule.

We are extremely grateful to our families, friends, neighbors and co-workers who have encouraged us over these past years. We appreciate the sharing of their favorite recipes and their comments and suggestions on recipes we passed their way.

To our husbands, Frank and Len, we extend our deepest thanks for their continuing support and encouragement.

Happy Cooking,
Irene & Verna

BREADS, BUNS, MUFFINS & LOAVES

Savor the incomparable aroma and
texture of good homemade bread.
A simple meal of soup and salad becomes
a feast with the addition of fresh-from-
the-oven yeast or quick breads. Enriched
with spices, fruit and vegetables, muffins
and loaves provide satisfying treats.

WHOLE-WHEAT BREAD

TRADITIONAL FLAVOR AND AROMA — JUST LIKE GRANDMA'S

1 tsp.	sugar	5 mL
½ cup	warm water	125 mL
2 tbsp.	yeast (2 envelopes, 2 x 7 g)	30 mL
1¾ cup	scalded milk, cooled to room temperature	425 mL
½ cup	sugar	125 mL
3 tbsp.	shortening	45 mL
1 tbsp.	molasses	15 mL
1 tsp.	salt	5 mL
2	eggs, beaten	2
4 cups	whole-wheat flour	1 L
3 cups	white flour	750 mL
1	egg	1
1 tbsp.	water	15 mL

- In a small bowl, dissolve 1 tsp. (5 mL) sugar in ½ cup (125 mL) water and sprinkle yeast over. Let sit for 8 minutes.
- Pour the milk into a large mixing bowl; add sugar, shortening, molasses, salt and 2 eggs. Mix well. Add the yeast mixture. Mix well.
- Add 2 cups (500 mL) of whole-wheat flour. Beat until smooth.
- Gradually add the remaining flour, until a soft dough is formed.
- Place dough on a floured surface and knead for 10 minutes, or until dough is smooth and elastic.
- Place dough in a large greased bowl. Cover and let rise until double in size, about 1 hour. Punch down and let rise again until double. Punch down and let rest for 15 minutes.
- To make loaves, divide dough into thirds. Form into loaves. Place in greased 5 x 9" (13 x 23 cm) loaf pans. Let rise until double in size. Brush the tops with a mixture of 1 egg and 1 tbsp. (15 mL) of water.
- Bake at 375°F (190°C) for 40 minutes. Turn out on wire racks to cool.

* Grease only the bottom of the loaf pans leaving the sides as a surface for batter to cling to while rising, so the loaves will form a rounded top.

NOTE   To make buns or small loaves reduce the baking time accordingly.

YIELD   ***3 LOAVES***

WHOLE-WHEAT BREAD/BUNS

A WHOLE ORANGE ADDED TO WHOLE-WHEAT BREAD KEEPS THE BREAD MOIST
AND GIVES A PLEASANT AROMA WHILE BAKING

½ cup	mashed potatoes	125 mL
½ cup	margarine	125 mL
⅓ cup	sugar	75 mL
2 cups	scalded milk, cooled to room temperature	500 mL
2	eggs	2
1 tsp.	baking powder	5 mL
½ tsp.	salt	2 mL
½ tsp.	baking soda	2 mL
¼ cup	honey	60 mL
1	orange (seed orange; chop, rind and all, in a food processor)	1
2 cups	white flour	500 mL
2 tbsp.	instant yeast (2 envelopes, 2 x 7g)	30 mL
5-6 cups	whole-wheat flour	1.25-1.5 L
1	egg	1
1 tbsp.	water	15 mL

- In a large bowl combine potatoes, margarine, sugar and milk. Mix well.
- Add eggs, baking powder, salt, soda, honey and orange. Mix well.
- In a small bowl combine the white flour and yeast. Add to the milk mixture. Beat well.
- Add the whole-wheat flour, 1 cup (250 mL) at a time, mixing well after each addition. When batter becomes too stiff to mix, remove from bowl and knead on a floured surface. Continue to add flour until dough comes away from hands and becomes smooth. Grease bowl and return dough to it. Grease top of dough. Cover with a clean tea towel.
- Let rise in a warm place until double in bulk, about 1 hour.
- Knead down. Shape into loaves, mini-loaves or buns. Place in greased baking pans. Let rise in a warm place until double in bulk. For a shiny crust, brush tops with an egg and water mixture, after dough rises.
- Bake at 350°F (180°C), about 30 minutes for loaves, 15-20 minutes for mini loaves and buns, or until the crust sounds hollow.

YIELD   *3, 5 X 9" (2 L) LOAVES, OR 20, 2½ X 4" (6 X 10 CM) MINI LOAVES*

WHITE BREAD

SERVE WARM AND BUTTERED WITH A HEARTY BOWL OF SOUP

1 tsp.	sugar	5 mL
½ cup	warm water	125 mL
1 tbsp.	yeast (1 envelope, 7 g)	15 mL
1½ cups	water	375 mL
½ cup	milk	125 mL
3 tbsp.	margarine	45 mL
3 tbsp.	sugar	45 mL
2 tsp.	salt	10 mL
1	egg, beaten	1
7 cups	flour	1.75 L
1	egg	1
1 tbsp.	water	15 mL

- In a large bowl, dissolve 1 tsp. (5 mL) sugar in ½ cup (125 mL) warm water. Sprinkle yeast over. Let sit for 8 minutes.
- In a saucepan, combine 1½ cups (375 mL) water, milk and margarine. Warm over low heat until margarine melts. Add to yeast mixture.
- Stir in 3 tbsp. (45 mL) sugar, salt and egg. Add 2 cups (500 mL) of flour. Beat until smooth.
- Gradually add remaining flour until a soft dough forms.
- Turn dough out onto a floured surface. Knead until smooth and elastic.
- Place dough in a large greased bowl. Cover and let rise until double in size, about 1 hour. Punch down and let rise again. Punch down and let rest for 15 minutes.
- Shape into loaves. Place in greased loaf pans. Let rise until double in size. Brush loaves with a mixture of 1 egg and 1 tbsp. (15 mL) of water.
- Bake at 375°F (190°C) for 40-45 minutes, or until golden brown. Turn out on wire racks to cool.

YIELD   *3 MEDIUM LOAVES OR 2 LARGE LOAVES*

CHERRY TRIANGLES

FROM BABA, TO US, TO YOU!

⅔ cup	milk, scalded	150 mL
1 tbsp.	active dry yeast (1 envelope, 7 g)	15 mL
1 cup	butter	250 mL
2½ cups	flour	625 mL
4	egg yolks, lightly beaten	4
2 x 19 oz.	cans cherry pie filling	2 x 540 mL
2 tbsp.	quick-cooking tapioca	30 mL
	butter icing	
	chopped walnuts	

- Cool milk to lukewarm. Add yeast. Let sit for 8 minutes .
- In a mixing bowl, with a pastry blender, cut butter into flour. Add yeast mixture and egg yolks. Mix thoroughly.
- Turn dough out onto a floured surface. Knead about a dozen times. Divide dough into 2 parts. Roll out 1 part to cover the surface of an ungreased 10 x 15" (25 x 38 cm) jelly roll pan.
- In a mixing bowl, combine pie filling with tapioca. Mix well. Spread pie filling evenly over dough.
- Roll out remaining dough to fit over the top of the pie filling. Pinch the edges of the dough together. Cut a slit in the top crust to allow steam to escape. Set aside in a warm place and let rise for 15 minutes.
- Bake at 350°F (180°C) for 50 minutes, or until golden brown. Cool.
- Ice with butter icing and sprinkle with walnuts.
- Cut into 24 squares and then cut each square diagonally.

YIELD   **48 CHERRY TRIANGLES**

PUMPKIN BABKA

A SPECIAL TREAT AT A UKRAINIAN EASTER FEAST, THIS DELICATE, FLAVORFUL
BREAD IS DELICIOUS WITH SALADS AND SOUPS

½ cup	warm water	125 mL
2 tsp.	sugar	10 mL
2 tbsp.	yeast (2 envelopes, 2 x 7 g)	30 mL
1 cup	scalded milk	250 mL
6 cups	flour	1.5 L
6	eggs	6
1 tsp.	salt	5 mL
½ cup	sugar	125 mL
½ cup	melted butter	125 mL
⅔ cup	mashed pumpkin	150 mL
½ cup	orange juice	125 mL
2 tbsp.	orange rind	30 mL
1 cup	raisins	250 mL

- In a small container, combine water and sugar. Sprinkle yeast on top. Let sit for 8 minutes.
- Cool scalded milk to room temperature.
- In a small mixing bowl, combine the milk and 1 cup (250 mL) of the flour. Beat well. Add the yeast mixture. Beat until well combined. Let mixture sit until light and bubbly, about 20 minutes.
- In a large mixing bowl, beat the eggs until light and fluffy. Add the salt, sugar, melted butter, pumpkin, orange juice and rind. Beat.
- Add the yeast mixture to the egg mixture. Combine well. Add the remaining flour gradually, with the raisins, while continuing to beat. Knead either manually for about 10 minutes or by machine for 5 minutes. Dough will not be stiff. It will be very soft.
- Place dough in a greased bowl. Cover with a tea towel and let rise in a warm room until double in size, about 1 hour. Punch down and let rise again until double in size.
- Prepare empty 1 lb. (500 g) coffee cans or 19 oz. (540 mL) cans for baking pans. Grease the insides of the cans well and then sprinkle insides with flour or fine bread crumbs.
- Fill the cans only ⅓ full with soft dough. Let rise until dough reaches the tops of the cans.

10

PUMPKIN BABKA

(CONTINUED)

- Bake at 350°F (180°C) for 10 minutes. Turn oven down to 300°F (150°C) and continue to bake for another 20 minutes, or until golden brown. Let cool for 10 minutes. Remove from cans.

VARIATION   Substitute mixed glacé fruit for raisins. Coat raisins or fruit with flour to prevent settling and sticking together.

YIELD   **8 MINI LOAVES (19 OZ. CAN SIZE)**

See photograph on page 87.

OVERNIGHT CINNAMON PULL-APARTS

GUARANTEED TO DISAPPEAR WITH THE MORNING COFFEE OR JUICE

½ x 3 lb.	pkg. of frozen white dinner roll dough	½ x 1.3 kg
½ x 4 oz.	pkg. butterscotch instant pudding mix	½ x 113 g
¾ cup	butter, softened	175 mL
1 cup	brown sugar	250 mL
2 tsp.	cinnamon	10 mL
¼ cup	nuts (optional)	60 mL
¼ cup	glacé cherries (optional)	60 mL

- Late in the evening, place frozen dinner roll dough in a greased 10" (25 cm) bundt pan.
- Sprinkle pudding mix over dough.
- Combine butter, brown sugar and cinnamon. Spread evenly over dough.
- If desired, sprinkle with nuts and cherries.
- Cover with foil. Let sit overnight at room temperature.
- In the morning, bake at 350°F (180°C) for 30 minutes.
- Cool in pan for 5 minutes before turning out and serving.

YIELD   **12-15 SERVINGS**

CHEESE BREAD/BUNS

BE CREATIVE — TRY A VARIETY OF INTERESTING SHAPES WITH
THIS TASTY BASIC CHEESE DOUGH RECIPE

½ cup	warm water	125 mL
½ tsp.	sugar	2 mL
1 tbsp.	yeast (1 envelope, 7 g)	15 mL
2 cups	warm water	500 mL
¼ cup	sugar	60 mL
1½ tsp.	salt	7 mL
2	eggs, beaten	2
¼ cup	oil	60 mL
6 cups	flour	1.5 L
2 cups	grated Cheddar cheese	500 mL

- Place ½ cup (125 mL) of warm water in a small bowl. Stir in ½ tsp. (2 mL) sugar. Sprinkle yeast on top of water. Set aside for 10 minutes.
- Pour 2 cups (500 mL) of warm water into a large mixing bowl; add ¼ cup (60 mL) sugar, salt, eggs and oil. Mix well. Add the yeast mixture. Mix well.
- Add 2 cups (500 mL) of flour and beat until smooth.
- Combine 1 cup (250 mL) of flour with the grated cheese. Add to the batter. Mix well.
- Gradually add the remaining 3 cups (750 mL) of flour. Work in flour with a wooden spoon or with your hands as the dough stiffens. Place dough on a floured surface and knead until it is smooth and elastic.
- Place dough in a greased bowl. Cover and let rise in a warm place until double in size, about 1 hour. Punch down and let rise again until double in size. Punch down and let dough rest for 15 minutes. Form into buns or bread as desired. Let rise until double in size.
- Bake at 375°F (190°C) until golden brown. The baking time depends on the size of pans used. Regular loaves take 30-40 minutes; smaller loaves or buns take 15-20 minutes to bake.

YIELD   *3 LOAVES*

CHEESE BREAD/BUNS

(CONTINUED)

VARIATION   To shape loaves into Kolach, a braided ring-shaped bread, pictured on page 33, take ⅓ of dough; divide into 9 equal pieces. Roll 2 pieces in a cylindrical shape to 8" (20 cm). Place the 2 lengths side by side. Starting from the centre, twine dough from left to right to form a rope-like twist. Position the twisted dough into a circle, leaving a small space in the centre. Cut the ends at an angle and join together by pinching. Take a third piece of dough and roll into a cylindrical shape long enough to enclose the twined circle. Repeat with the remaining dough.

See photograph on page 33.

CHEESE CORN STICKS

ENJOY THIS CORNBREAD BAKED SOUTHERN STYLE OR AS MUFFINS

½ cup	flour	125 mL
½ cup	cornmeal	125 mL
2 tsp.	baking powder	10 mL
¼ tsp.	salt	1 mL
½ cup	milk	125 mL
1	egg, beaten	1
3 tbsp.	vegetable oil	45 mL
½ cup	grated Cheddar cheese	125 mL

- Preheat oven to 425°F (220°C). While preparing the batter, place a cast-iron corn stick pan in oven to heat.
- In a mixing bowl, combine flour, cornmeal, baking powder and salt.
- In a small bowl, combine milk, egg and vegetable oil. Mix well. Add to dry ingredients. Stir just until dry ingredients are moistened.
- Remove hot corn stick pan from oven. Brush generously with vegetable oil. Spoon batter into pan. Sprinkle cheese on top.
- Bake for 8-10 minutes, or until lightly browned.

VARIATION   Bake in greased, medium muffin tins at 425°F (220°C) for 12 minutes.

YIELD   ***10 CORN STICKS OR 6 MUFFINS***

See photograph on page 139.

GARLIC CHEDDAR LOAF

THE PERFECT ACCOMPANIMENT FOR A BARBECUE!

1	loaf French bread	1
¾ cup	butter	175 mL
2 cups	grated Cheddar cheese	500 mL
¼ cup	sour cream	60 mL
3	garlic cloves, crushed	3
1 tbsp.	chopped fresh parsley	15 mL
1 tbsp.	chopped fresh dill	15 mL

- Slice the French loaf in half lengthwise.
- In a bowl, combine the remaining ingredients. Mix well.
- Spread cheese mixture over the 2 halves of bread. Place bread on a cookie sheet. Bake at 350°F (180°C) for 12 minutes, or until bubbly.
- Slice crosswise. Serve warm.

YIELD   *1 LOAF*

ONION AND CHEESE BREAD

SERVE WARM WITH A BOWL OF CHILI OR WITH TACO SOUP, PAGE 64. SUPERB!

½ cup	chopped onion	125 mL
1 tbsp.	margarine	15 mL
1½ cups	flour	375 mL
1 tbsp.	baking powder	15 mL
½ tsp.	salt	2 mL
3 tbsp.	butter	45 mL
1 cup	grated sharp Cheddar cheese	250 mL
1	egg, beaten	1
½ cup	milk	125 mL

ONION AND CHEESE BREAD
(CONTINUED)

- In a small skillet, fry onion in margarine until onion is translucent. Set aside.
- In a mixing bowl, combine flour, baking powder and salt. Cut in butter until mixture is crumbly. Stir in ½ of the cheese.
- In a small bowl, combine egg, milk and onion mixture. Add to flour mixture. Mix. Pat soft dough into a greased 5 x 9" (13 x 23 cm) loaf pan or 8" (20 cm) round pan. Sprinkle with the remaining half of the cheese.
- Bake at 400°F (200°C) for 25 minutes, or until golden brown.

YIELD   *1 LOAF*

HERBED BEER BREAD

A QUICK FLAVORFUL BREAD THAT IS EASY FOR ANYONE TO MAKE *try adding cheese to dry*

2¾ cups	flour	675 mL
2 tbsp.	sugar	30 mL
2 tbsp.	baking powder	30 mL
1 tsp.	salt	5 mL
¼ tsp.	oregano	1 mL
¼ tsp.	thyme	1 mL
¼ tsp.	dried dillweed	1 mL
12 oz.	can of beer	355 mL
	butter	

- In a large bowl, stir together the first 7 ingredients.
- Add beer. Mix well.
- Place batter in a 4 x 8" (10 x 20 cm) greased loaf pan.
- Bake at 375°F (190°C) for 50 minutes, or until golden on top. Brush the top with butter. *try 40 mins first - 50 not enough*
- Let stand in pan for 5 minutes before turning out onto a cooling rack.

NOTE   Beer Bread mix makes a nice gift from the kitchen. Combine the first 7 ingredients. Place in an airtight container. Include directions for adding beer and baking. Decorate container with gift wrap or leftover fabric and ribbons or bows.

YIELD   *1 LOAF*

TOMATO BASIL BREAD

THIS SAVORY LOAF IS IDEAL SERVED WITH SOUPS, SALADS OR MAIN COURSES

½ cup	butter	125 mL
1 tbsp.	tomato paste	15 mL
1 tbsp.	brown sugar	15 mL
2	eggs	2
2 cups	flour	500 mL
1 tsp.	baking powder	5 mL
1 tsp.	baking soda	5 mL
1 tsp.	crumbled dried basil	5 mL
½ cup	tomato juice	125 mL
1 cup	grated Cheddar cheese	250 mL

- In a mixing bowl, beat butter, tomato paste, sugar and eggs until light and fluffy.
- In a small bowl, combine flour, baking powder, baking soda and basil.
- Gradually add dry ingredients to butter mixture alternately with tomato juice. Fold in cheese.
- Spread batter in a greased 5 x 9" (13 x 22 cm) loaf pan.
- Bake at 350°F (180°C) for 45 minutes, or until a skewer inserted in the centre comes out clean.
- Cool on a wire rack for 5 minutes. Turn out of loaf pan. Let cool completely. Wrap and refrigerate for 12 hours before serving.

YIELD   1 LOAF

See photograph on page 121.

WHOLE-WHEAT SODA BREAD

SERVE THIS HEARTY, COARSE-TEXTURED LOAF WITH SOUPS AND STEWS

1 cup	all-purpose flour	250 mL
1 tsp.	baking powder	5 mL
1 tsp.	baking soda	5 mL
½ tsp.	salt	2 mL
2 tbsp.	sugar	30 mL
2 cups	whole-wheat flour	500 mL
1½ cups	buttermilk	375 mL
1 tbsp.	melted butter	15 mL

- In a large mixing bowl, combine the all-purpose flour, baking powder, baking soda, salt and sugar. Add the whole-wheat flour. Mix well.
- Add buttermilk. Mix only until dry ingredients are moistened.
- Turn dough onto a floured surface. Knead gently for about 2 minutes, or until dough is smooth and ingredients are well mixed.
- Shape dough into a ball. Place on a lightly greased cookie sheet. Shape dough into a 7-8" (18-20 cm) circle about 1½" (4 cm) in height.
- With the use of a floured knife, mark the circle of dough into quarters by cutting halfway through to the bottom.
- Bake at 375°F (190°C) for 40 minutes, or until the loaf sounds hollow when tapped.
- Brush top of bread with melted butter. Cool on a wire rack.

YIELD   1 LOAF

See photograph on page 69.

OLD-FASHIONED NUT BREAD

A FAVORITE THAT HAS RETAINED ITS POPULARITY OVER TIME!

1 cup	sugar	250 mL
1	egg	1
2 cups	flour	500 mL
½ tsp.	salt	2 mL
4 tsp.	baking powder	20 mL
1 cup	milk	250 mL
1 cup	raisins	250 mL
1 cup	chopped walnuts	250 mL

- In a mixing bowl, beat sugar and egg.
- In a small bowl, combine the flour, salt and baking powder. Add dry ingredients to the egg mixture alternately with the milk.
- Add raisins and walnuts. Mix until well combined.
- Pour into a greased 5 x 9" (13 x 23 cm) loaf pan.
- Let rise for 20 minutes.
- Bake at 350°F (180°C) for 40 minutes, or until a toothpick inserted in the center comes out clean.

YIELD   *1 LOAF*

APPLE RAISIN MUFFINS

MOIST AND HEARTY, IDEAL FOR LUNCHES AND SNACKS

1 cup	white flour	250 mL
1 cup	whole-wheat flour	250 mL
1 cup	sugar	250 mL
2 tsp.	baking soda	10 mL
2 tsp.	cinnamon	10 mL
¼ tsp.	salt	1 mL
3	apples, grated	3
½ cup	raisins	125 mL
½ cup	chopped nuts	125 mL
½ cup	coconut	125 mL
3	eggs	3
1 cup	vegetable oil	250 mL
2 tsp.	vanilla	10 mL

- In a large mixing bowl combine flours, sugar, baking soda, cinnamon and salt.
- Add apples, raisins, nuts and coconut. Mix well.
- In a small bowl combine eggs, oil and vanilla. Mix well.
- Pour liquid ingredients over dry ingredients. Mix only until dry ingredients are moistened.
- Fill greased large muffin tins ⅔ full.
- Bake at 350°F (180°C) for 20-25 minutes.

YIELD   *12 LARGE MUFFINS*

BANANA CHOCOLATE CHIP MUFFINS
GUARANTEED TO BE A HIT FOR LUNCHES!

⅔ cup	vegetable oil	150 mL
1 cup	sugar	250 mL
2	eggs	2
2	ripe bananas, mashed	2
2 cups	flour	500 mL
1 tsp.	baking soda	5 mL
½ tsp.	salt	2 mL
1 tsp.	cinnamon	5 mL
½ cup	buttermilk*	125 mL
2 cups	chocolate chips	500 mL

- In a small mixing bowl, beat together oil, sugar, eggs and mashed bananas.
- In a large mixing bowl, combine flour, baking soda, salt and cinnamon. Make a well in dry ingredients. Add oil mixture alternately with buttermilk. Add chocolate chips. Fold in gently.
- Fill greased medium-sized muffin tins ⅔ full. Bake at 375°F (190°C) for 20 minutes, or until a toothpick inserted in the center comes out clean.

* Sour cream or yogurt may be substituted for the buttermilk.

YIELD   *24 MUFFINS*

BRAN MUFFINS

GREAT FOR WHEN YOU WANT ONLY A DOZEN AT A TIME!

1½ cups	natural bran OR bran cereal	375 mL
1 cup	buttermilk	250 mL
⅓ cup	vegetable oil	75 mL
1	egg	1
⅔ cup	brown sugar	150 mL
1 tsp.	vanilla	5 mL
1 cup	flour	250 mL
½ tsp.	salt	2 mL
1 tsp.	baking soda	5 mL
1 tsp.	baking powder	5 mL
⅔ cup	raisins	150 mL

- In a small bowl, combine bran and buttermilk.
- In a mixing bowl, combine oil, egg, brown sugar and vanilla. Add bran mixture.
- In a separate bowl, combine dry ingredients and raisins. Add to bran mixture. Mix only until blended.
- Fill greased medium-sized muffin tins ¾ full.
- Bake at 375°F (190°C) for 18 minutes, or until muffins spring back when lightly touched.

YIELD   *12 MUFFINS*

BLUEBERRY YOGURT BRAN MUFFINS

AN UNUSUAL BUT WINNING COMBINATION OF FLAVORS

2 cups	yogurt	500 mL
2 tsp.	baking soda	10 mL
1 cup	brown sugar	250 mL
2	eggs	2
1 cup	vegetable oil	250 mL
2 cups	bran	500 mL
2 tsp.	vanilla	10 mL
2 cups	flour	500 mL
4 tsp.	baking powder	20 mL
¼ tsp.	salt	1 mL
1 cup	blueberries	250 mL

- In a small mixing bowl, combine yogurt and baking soda. Set aside. This mixture will rise.
- In a large mixing bowl, combine brown sugar, eggs and oil. Mix well. Stir in bran and vanilla.
- In a separate bowl, combine flour, baking powder and salt.
- Add dry ingredients to bran mixture alternately with yogurt. Fold in blueberries.
- Fill greased medium-sized muffin tins ⅔ full. Bake at 350°F (180°C) for 25-30 minutes.

YIELD   **24 MUFFINS**

STREUSEL COFFEE CAKE

GREAT FOR MORNING COFFEE BREAK OR FOR DESSERT AFTER A LIGHT LUNCH

2½ cups	flour	625 mL
¾ cup	brown sugar	175 mL
⅔ cup	butter	150 mL
½ tsp.	baking powder	2 mL
½ tsp.	baking soda	2 mL
¾ cup	evaporated milk	175 mL
1 tbsp.	lemon juice	15 mL
1	egg	1
1 tsp.	almond extract	5 mL
1½ cups	prepared pie filling*	375 mL
⅓ cup	sliced almonds	75 mL

- In a mixing bowl, combine the flour and sugar. With a pastry blender, cut in butter until mixture is crumbly. Set aside ½ cup (125 mL) for topping. To the remainder of the crumbs, add the baking powder and baking soda.
- In a small bowl, combine the evaporated milk and lemon juice. Stir well. Let sit for 5 minutes, until mixture thickens. Add egg and almond extract. Beat well.
- Add egg mixture to the crumb mixture. Stir until just moistened. Spread batter into a greased 9" (23 cm) springform pan and 1" (2.5 cm) up the sides of the pan.
- Drop spoonfuls of a your favorite flavor of pie filling onto the batter. Sprinkle the ½ cup (125 mL) of reserved crumbs on top. Sprinkle with almonds.
- Bake at 350°F (180°C) for 55 minutes. Serve warm or cooled.

* Try your favorite fruit fillings. For infinite variations, combine fillings, e.g., apple-raisin, peach-blueberry; raisin-peach, apple-raspberry, etc.

YIELD   *8 SERVINGS*

CHOCOLATE CHIP COFFEE RING

A COFFEE CAKE WITH A DIFFERENT FLAVOR — CHOCOLATE CHIPS!

1 cup	sugar	250 mL
½ cup	butter	125 mL
2	eggs	2
2 cups	flour	500 mL
1 tsp.	baking powder	5 mL
1 tsp.	baking soda	5 mL
1 cup	sour cream	250 mL
1 tsp.	vanilla	5 mL
1 cup	chocolate chips	250 mL
¼ cup	butter	60 mL
½ cup	brown sugar	125 mL
½ cup	flour	125 mL
1 tbsp.	cocoa	15 mL
½ cup	chopped pecans	125 mL

- In a large mixing bowl, beat sugar and butter until light and fluffy. Add the eggs. Beat.
- In a small mixing bowl, combine the flour, baking powder and baking soda. Add to egg mixture alternately with sour cream. Add vanilla and ½ of the chocolate chips. Mix well.
- Pour the batter into a greased 9" (23 cm) bundt pan. Sprinkle the remaining chocolate chips on top.
- In a small bowl, combine the butter, brown sugar, flour, cocoa and pecans. Mix until crumbly. Sprinkle on top of chocolate chips.
- Bake at 350°F (180°C) for 60 minutes, or until cake pulls away from sides of pan. Let sit for 10 minutes before turning out onto a wire rack.

YIELD   *12-15 GENEROUS SERVINGS*

ORANGE COFFEE CAKE

THE FLAVOR AND AROMA OF THE ORANGE MAKES THIS COFFEE CAKE SPECIAL

2 cups	flour	500 mL
1 tsp.	cinnamon	5 mL
1 tsp.	baking powder	5 mL
¼ tsp.	nutmeg	1 mL
1 tsp.	baking soda	5 mL
pinch	salt	pinch
1 cup	sugar	250 mL
1	egg, beaten	1
1 cup	milk	250 mL
½ cup	vegetable oil	125 mL
1	orange (seed orange; chop, rind and all, in a food processor)	1
⅓ cup	brown sugar	75 mL
¼ cup	margarine	60 mL
1 cup	chopped nuts	250 mL

VANILLA GLAZE:

¾ cup	icing sugar	175 mL
1 tbsp.	milk	15 mL
½ tsp.	vanilla	2 mL

- In a mixing bowl, combine flour, cinnamon, baking powder, nutmeg, baking soda, salt and sugar.
- Add egg, milk, oil and orange. Mix well.
- Pour into a greased and floured 9 x 13" (23 x 33 cm) pan or 10" (25 cm) bundt pan.
- Combine sugar, margarine and nuts. Sprinkle over batter.
- Bake at 350°F (180°C) for 30 minutes.
- Combine glaze ingredients. Drizzle over warm cake.

YIELD   *12 SERVINGS*

RHUBARB CAKE

THIS DELICIOUS MOIST CAKE IS OFTEN CALLED LUNAR CAKE BECAUSE
OF ITS IRREGULAR TOP

✓ 1 cup	brown sugar	250 mL
✓ ½ cup	margarine	125 mL
✓ 1 cup	milk – *buttermilk*	250 mL
✓ 1 tsp.	baking soda	5 mL
✓ 1 tsp.	vanilla	5 mL
✓ ¼ tsp.	salt	2 mL
✓ 1	egg	1
✓ 2 cups	flour	500 mL
2⅔ – 1½ cups	finely chopped rhubarb	375 mL
1 tbsp.	butter	15 mL
¼ ✓ ½ cup	brown sugar	125 mL
✓ ½ tsp.	cinnamon	2 mL
½ tsp.	nutmeg	2 mL

- In a mixing bowl, cream together brown sugar and margarine.
- Add milk, baking soda, vanilla, salt, egg and flour. Mix well. *dry & wet alternately*
- Stir in rhubarb.
- Turn batter into a greased 9 x 13" (23 x 33 cm) pan.
- Combine the remaining ingredients until crumbly. Spread evenly over batter.
- Bake at 350°F (180°C) for 1 hour. *–try 35 mins first*

**SERVING
SUGGESTIONS**   Serve warm with ice cream or whipped cream.

YIELD   *12-15 SERVINGS*

BRUNCHES & LUNCHES

Create enjoyable everyday lunches
and special-occasion brunches. Quick and
easy or lavish and luxurious, lunches
and brunches can be nourishing
family meals and delightful opportunities
for entertaining.

EGGS BENEDICT

SERVE ON SPECIAL OCCASIONS — IT DESERVES THAT RECOGNITION

2	English muffins, halved	2
	butter	
4	slices ham OR back bacon	4
4	poached eggs	4

HOLLANDAISE SAUCE:

3	egg yolks	3
2 tbsp.	lemon juice	30 mL
½ cup	cold butter	125 mL
1 tsp.	Dijon mustard (optional)	5 mL
	dash of cayenne pepper (optional)	

- Toast and butter muffin halves. Keep warm.
- In a skillet, fry ham or bacon.
- On each muffin half, place a piece of ham or bacon. Top with a poached egg.
- While preparing muffins, ham or bacon and eggs, prepare sauce. In a small saucepan, combine egg yolks and lemon juice. Add butter all at once. Cook over low heat stirring frequently until thickened. Spoon over poached eggs on muffins. Serve immediately.

NOTE	Do not overcook sauce as it will curdle. Remove from heat as soon as it is thickened. Try making the hollandaise in a microwave at low heat.
SERVING SUGGESTIONS	Serve as a brunch dish with a butter lettuce salad or fresh fruit.
YIELD	*4 SERVINGS*

CHEESE SOUFFLÉ

THIS, THE MOST POPULAR OF ALL SOUFFLÉS, IS A DELIGHT TO MAKE AND SERVE

2 tbsp.	margarine	30 mL
2 tbsp.	flour	30 mL
1 cup	skim milk	250 mL
½ lb.	Swiss cheese, grated	250 g
¼ tsp.	cayenne pepper (optional)	1 mL
6	eggs (at room temperature), separated	6
½ tsp.	cream of tartar	2 mL

- In a double boiler, melt margarine; stir in flour. Cook until well blended. Gradually add milk and cheese a little bit at a time. Cook and stir until mixture is thick and smooth. Stir in cayenne pepper, if using. Cool for a minimum of 15 minutes.
- Add slightly beaten egg yolks, 1 at a time, to cooled cheese sauce.
- In a large glass bowl, beat egg whites until foamy. Sprinkle with cream of tartar. Continue to beat until stiff.
- Spoon 1 cup (250 mL) of the egg whites into the cheese mixture. Blend well. Gradually add cheese mixture to egg whites, folding until well mixed.
- With aluminum foil, make a collar to extend the height of a 2-quart (2 L) soufflé dish by about 2" (5 cm).
- Pour cheese mixture into ungreased soufflé dish. With a spatula, run a groove in the batter about 1½" (4 cm) deep and about 1¼" (3 cm) in from the edge of the dish. This will produce a crown or "high hat" finish to the soufflé.
- Bake at 350°F (180°C) for 30 minutes, or until firm. Serve at once.

NOTE   Some cooks prefer to grease the soufflé dish while others say the ungreased sides give the soufflé something to cling to and it rises higher. The sauce which is made in the double boiler can also be made in a glass container in a microwave. However, only cook it for short periods of time stirring frequently between cooking times. Experiment to see which method works best for you.

YIELD   *4 SERVINGS*

SALMON SOUFFLÉ

AN IMPRESSIVE ENTREÉ FOR A LUNCHEON

2 tbsp.	margarine	30 mL
2 tbsp.	flour	30 mL
1 cup	skim milk, scalded	250 mL
4	eggs, separated	4
¼ tsp.	salt	1 mL
¼ tsp.	pepper	1 mL
¼ tsp.	dry mustard	1 mL
½ tsp.	Worcestershire sauce	2 mL
7.5 oz.	can of salmon, drained	213 g
¼ tsp.	cream of tartar	1 mL

- In a saucepan over medium heat, melt margarine. Blend in flour with a wire whisk. Add hot milk. While stirring, cook until mixture is thick and smooth. Cool for at least 15 minutes.
- Add egg yolks, 1 at a time, to cooled white sauce. Add salt, pepper, dry mustard and Worcestershire sauce. Flake salmon and add. Mix well.
- In a large mixing bowl, beat egg whites until foamy. Sprinkle with cream of tartar. Continue to beat until stiff.
- Add 1 cup (250 mL) of egg whites to salmon mixture. Blend well. Gradually add salmon mixture to egg whites, folding until thoroughly mixed.
- Pour salmon mixture into an ungreased 2-quart (2 L) soufflé dish.
- Bake at 350°F (180°C) for 30 minutes, or until soufflé is firm. Serve immediately.

YIELD   **3-4 SERVINGS**

BRUNCH

Hash-Brown Quiche, page 36
Salad of the Gods, page 76
Cheese Bread/Buns, page 12

OVEN-BAKED OMELET

A GREAT BREAKFAST WITH WHOLE-WHEAT TOAST AND FRESH FRUIT

¼ cup	margarine, melted	60 mL
12	eggs	12
⅔ cup	sour cream	150 mL
½ cup	milk	125 mL
1 tsp.	salt	5 mL
⅓ cup	chopped green onions	75 mL

- Spread margarine in a 9½" (24 cm) deep-dish pie plate.
- In a mixing bowl, beat eggs, sour cream, milk and salt. Stir in onion. Pour into the baking dish.
- Bake at 325°F (160°C) for 30 minutes, until eggs are set but still moist.

VARIATION   Add a Mexican flavor, serve with chunky salsa, mild or hot.

YIELD   **6 SERVINGS**

ZUCCHINI TOMATO IMPOSSIBLE PIE

A LUNCHEON DISH IN SUMMER WHEN VEGETABLES ARE YOUNG AND TENDER!

2 cups	chopped zucchini	500 mL
1 cup	chopped tomato	250 mL
½ cup	chopped onion	125 mL
½ cup	grated Parmesan cheese	125 mL
1½ cups	milk	375 mL
¾ cup	biscuit baking mix	175 mL
½ tsp.	each salt and pepper	2 mL

- In a greased 10" (25 cm) quiche dish, distribute zucchini, tomato and onion evenly. Sprinkle with cheese.
- In a small bowl, combine milk, biscuit mix, salt and pepper. Whisk until well blended. Pour over the vegetables.
- Bake at 400°F (200°C) for 30 minutes, or until a knife inserted in the center comes out clean. Cool for 5 minutes before slicing and serving.

VARIATION   Substitute other vegetables for zucchini and tomato.

YIELD   **6 SERVINGS**

CRUSTLESS QUICHE

NO CRUST — FEWER CALORIES, GREAT FLAVOR AND A GREAT TIME SAVER!

½ cup	chopped ham	125 mL
½	green pepper, chopped	½
½ cup	sliced fresh mushrooms	125 mL
1	medium tomato, chopped	1
2	green onions, chopped	2
3	eggs, slightly beaten	3
1 cup	half and half cream	250 mL
½ tsp.	salt	2 mL
½ tsp.	pepper	2 mL
¼ tsp.	nutmeg	1 mL
¼ tsp.	dry mustard	1 mL
1 cup	shredded mozzarella cheese	250 mL

- In a greased 9" (23 cm) pie plate, distribute the ham, green pepper, mushrooms, tomato and onions evenly.
- In a small bowl, combine the remaining ingredients, except the cheese. Pour over the vegetables. Sprinkle the cheese on top.
- Bake at 375°F (190°C) for 35 minutes, or until a knife inserted in the center comes out clean.

YIELD   5-6 SERVINGS

HASH-BROWN QUICHE

WITH A SALAD, THIS IS A COMPLETE MEAL-IN-ONE!

1 lb.	frozen hash-brown potatoes	500 g
⅓ cup	melted butter	75 mL
1 cup	shredded Cheddar cheese	250 mL
1 cup	shredded Swiss cheese	250 mL
1 cup	diced ham	250 mL
4	eggs	4
½ cup	half and half cream	125 mL
¼ tsp.	salt	1 mL
¼ tsp.	pepper	1 mL

HASH-BROWN QUICHE
(CONTINUED)

- Slightly thaw hash-brown potatoes. Remove excess moisture. Press potatoes into a greased 9 x 13" (23 x 33 cm) pan.
- Brush melted butter over potatoes. Bake at 425°F (220°C) for 20 minutes. Remove from oven and lower temperature to 350°F (180°C).
- Sprinkle cheeses and ham evenly over the crust.
- Beat together eggs and cream. Add salt and pepper. Pour over cheeses and ham.
- Bake at 350°F (180°C) for 35 minutes, or until set.

YIELD   **6 SERVINGS**

See photograph on page 33.

HAM 'N' CHEESE QUICHE
AN OLD STANDBY TOO GOOD TO FORGET

1	9" (23 cm) unbaked pie shell	1
1½ cups	cubed cooked ham	375 mL
2 cups	grated Swiss cheese	500 mL
3	eggs	3
2	green onions, chopped	2
1 tsp.	Dijon mustard	5 mL
¼ tsp.	salt	1 mL
1 cup	milk	250 mL
2 tbsp.	grated Parmesan cheese	30 mL

- Prepare the pie shell.
- Distribute the ham and cheese evenly in the pie shell.
- In a small bowl, combine the eggs, onions, mustard, salt and milk. Pour over the ham and cheese.
- Sprinkle with Parmesan cheese.
- Bake at 375°F (190°C) for 30-35 minutes, or until set.

SERVING SUGGESTION   Serve with a tossed salad and accompanying fruit for brunch.

YIELD   **5-6 SERVINGS**

PASTA WITH COOL SEAFOOD SAUCE

THE DELIGHTFUL CONTRAST OF COOL FRESH SAUCE AND HOT PASTA MAKES
THIS A SUMMER FAVORITE

8 oz.	scallops	250 g
1 tbsp.	butter	15 mL
4 oz.	cooked crab meat, chopped	125 g
4	fresh tomatoes, diced	4
1	garlic clove, crushed	1
1 tsp.	dried basil	5 mL
¼ cup	grated Parmesan cheese	60 mL
¼ cup	olive oil	60 mL
1 tbsp.	lemon juice	15 mL
½ tsp.	salt	2 mL
½ tsp.	pepper	2 mL
8 oz.	linguine	250 g

- In a skillet, sauté scallops in butter for 3 minutes, or until opaque. Place in a mixing bowl. Add remaining ingredients, except linguine. Mix. Cover. Refrigerate.
- Prepare the linguine according to package directions. Drain and toss the hot linguine immediately with the cool seafood mixture. Serve.

VARIATION   Heat the sauce and serve the hot seafood sauce over hot pasta.

YIELD   **4 SERVINGS**

PIZZA

FROM SCRATCH IN LESS THAN AN HOUR, PREPARE THE TOPPINGS
WHILE THE DOUGH RISES

1 tbsp.	yeast	15 mL
1 tsp.	sugar	5 mL
1 cup	warm water	250 mL
2½ cups	flour	625 mL
½ tsp.	salt	2 mL
3 tbsp.	vegetable oil	45 mL
	pizza OR tomato sauce	
	sliced meat (salami, pepperoni, ham)	
	sliced vegetables (onion, green pepper, mushrooms)	
	grated cheese	

- In a small bowl, dissolve the yeast and sugar in the warm water. Let sit for 10 minutes, or until double in size.
- In a mixing bowl, combine yeast mixture with flour, salt and oil. Knead until dough forms a smooth ball.
- Grease a large stainless steel mixing bowl. Roll the dough in the bowl until lightly coated with grease. Cover with a tea towel and place in an oven set at 200°F (100°C). Let dough rise in oven until double in size, about 20 minutes.
- Spread dough out evenly onto a greased 12" (30 cm) pizza pan, pressing dough up slightly at the edge.
- Spread pizza sauce on top of dough. Add meat, vegetables and cheese as desired.
- Bake at 400°F (200°C) for 20 minutes, or until underside of crust is golden brown.

VARIATIONS   Pizza can suit anyone's taste. Add chopped red or yellow peppers, steamed broccoli florets, snow peas, artichoke hearts, shrimp, crab, chopped black or green olives, jalapeño peppers, hot sauces, feta cheese, spinach, crushed garlic, chopped fresh basil, oregano, thyme. Your imagination is the only limit.

YIELD   *4-6 SERVINGS*

FRENCH LOAF PIZZA

A HIT WITH THE YOUNG CROWD OUT ON THE PATIO

1 lb.	Italian sausages	500 g
2	garlic cloves, chopped	2
1	medium onion, chopped	1
19 oz.	can tomatoes, drained, chopped	540 mL
5½ oz.	can tomato paste	156 mL
1 tbsp.	dried basil	15 mL
½ tsp.	dried ground oregano	2 mL
½ tsp.	pepper	2 mL
7 oz.	Mozzarella cheese, shredded	200 g
4 oz.	Cheddar cheese, grated	115 g
1	loaf French bread, unsliced	1

- In a skillet, brown the sausages. Remove with a slotted spoon. Keep warm. Drain off all but 1 tbsp. (15 mL) of drippings.
- In reserved drippings, sauté garlic and onions until soft. Add tomatoes, tomato paste, basil, oregano and pepper. Simmer for 15 minutes, stirring occasionally.
- In the meantime, slice off the top of the loaf of bread lengthwise. Scoop out the center of the loaf leaving a 1" (2.5 cm) shell.
- Spread half of the tomato mixture into the hollowed loaf. Layer the sausages over the tomatoes. Top with remaining tomato mixture. Sprinkle the cheeses on top. Replace the top of the loaf.
- Double wrap loaf in heavy aluminum foil. Place on a cookie sheet.
- Bake at 300°F (150°C) for 1½ hours. Remove from oven and let set for 20 minutes.
- To serve, cut loaf into 2" (5 cm) slices.

VARIATIONS Mushrooms, peppers, chopped olives or other vegetables, as desired, can be added along with the garlic and onions. For individual servings use crusty rolls in place of the French loaf. Reduce the required baking time by about ½ hour.

SERVING SUGGESTION Serve with a salad.

YIELD **1 STUFFED PIZZA LOAF OR 8 INDIVIDUAL STUFFED ROLLS.**

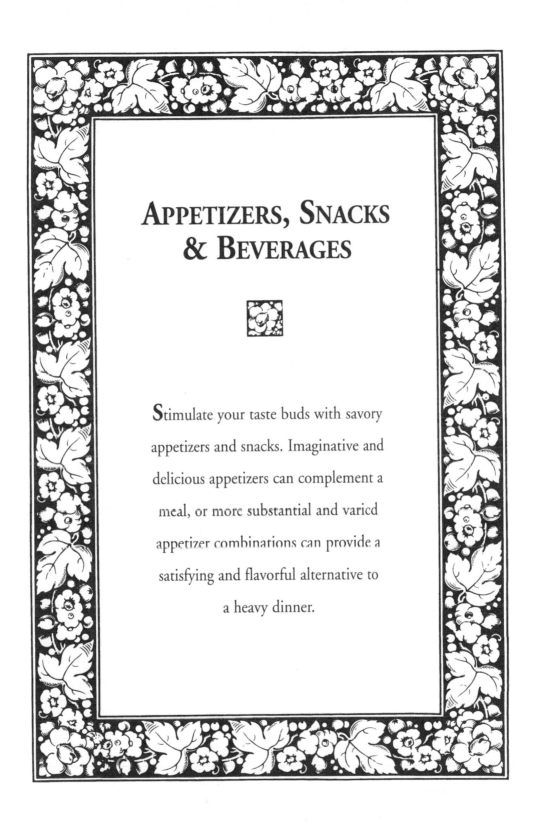

APPETIZERS, SNACKS & BEVERAGES

Stimulate your taste buds with savory
appetizers and snacks. Imaginative and
delicious appetizers can complement a
meal, or more substantial and varied
appetizer combinations can provide a
satisfying and flavorful alternative to
a heavy dinner.

BRANDIED CHEESE BALLS

QUICK, EASY, CONVENIENT — FOR EVERYDAY OR FOR GUESTS

2 x 8 oz.	pkgs. cream cheese	2 x 250 g
8 oz.	sharp Cheddar cheese, grated	250 g
2 tbsp.	brandy	30 mL
2 tsp.	Worcestershire sauce	10 mL
1 tbsp.	chopped green pepper	15 mL
1 tbsp.	chopped pimiento	15 mL
1 tbsp.	finely chopped green onion	15 mL
dash	Tabasco	dash
1 tbsp.	lemon juice	15 mL
	crushed pecans	

- Combine all ingredients, except pecans.
- Shape into 4 balls. Chill in refrigerator.
- Roll in crushed pecans.
- Freeze until required.

YIELD   *4 CHEESE BALLS*

CRAB CHEESE BALL

THE SAUCE IS WHAT MAKES THIS APPETIZER EXTRA SPECIAL

8 oz.	cream cheese	250 g
2 tbsp.	finely grated onion	30 mL
2 tsp.	Worcestershire sauce	10 mL
1 cup	flaked crabmeat	250 mL
½ cup	chili sauce	125 mL
2 tbsp.	horseradish	30 mL
1 tbsp.	lemon juice	15 mL

CRAB CHEESE BALL
(CONTINUED)

- Combine cheese, onion, Worcestershire sauce and crabmeat. Form into a ball. Wrap in waxed paper and chill.
- Combine chili sauce, horseradish and lemon juice. Mix well. Refrigerate.
- When ready to serve, place cheese ball in a shallow dish. Pour the chili horseradish sauce over. Serve with a variety of crackers.

YIELD   *1 CHEESE BALL, SERVES 15-20*

QUICK AND EASY ANTIPASTO
NO COOKING REQUIRED AND VERY FLAVORFUL

10 oz.	can mushroom pieces and stems, drained	284 mL
13 oz.	jar gherkins, drained, chopped	375 mL
13 oz.	jar salad olives, drained, chopped	375 mL
2 x 6.5 oz.	cans flaked white tuna in water, drained and rinsed	2 x 184 g
13 oz.	bottle hot ketchup	375 mL
13 oz.	bottle chili sauce	375 mL

- In a large mixing bowl combine all ingredients.
- Spoon antipasto into sterilized jars.
- Refrigerate or freeze until needed.

YIELD   *8 CUPS (2 L)*

JALAPEÑO TORTILLA ROLLS

AN EASY, PREPARE-IN-ADVANCE, ADAPTABLE APPETIZER FOR A LARGE GATHERING

8 oz.	cream cheese	250 g
¼ cup	finely chopped jalapeños OR mild green chilies	60 mL
¼ cup	finely chopped pecans	60 mL
¼ cup	chopped ripe olives	60 mL
¼ cup	finely chopped green onions	60 mL
¼ cup	chopped pimientos	60 mL
¼ tsp.	garlic powder	1 mL
8 x 8"	flour tortillas	8 x 20 cm

- In a mixing bowl, combine all ingredients except tortillas.
- Divide cheese mixture evenly among the tortillas. Spread cheese mixture over each tortilla completely covering to the edges. Roll each tortilla up jelly roll style.
- Wrap tortillas in plastic wrap. Refrigerate several hours or overnight.
- To serve, cut each tortilla roll into ½" (1.3 cm) rounds, and lay cut side down on a serving tray.

VARIATIONS   Use mild green chilies instead of jalapeños for a less spicy flavor.

YIELD   ***ABOUT 80 APPETIZERS***

See photograph on page 51.

SEAFOOD-STUFFED SHELLS

GREAT FINGER FOOD FOR A COCKTAIL PARTY

1 lb.	uncooked jumbo pasta shells	500 g
4 oz.	can cocktail shrimp, drained	113 g
8 oz.	crabmeat, chopped	250 g
4 oz.	Swiss cheese, shredded	115 g
½ cup	mayonnaise	125 mL
1	celery stalk, chopped	1
2	green onions, finely chopped	2
1 tbsp.	finely chopped pimiento	15 mL

SEAFOOD-STUFFED SHELLS
(CONTINUED)

- Cook the pasta shells according to package directions, until tender but firm. Drain. Rinse with cold water. Drain. Set shells aside, upside down so they drain well.
- In a bowl, combine the shrimp, crab and remaining ingredients.
- Gently spoon the seafood mixture into the drained shells. Cover and refrigerate until chilled. Serve.

YIELD   ***APPETIZERS FOR 20***

See photograph on page 51.

LAYERED SEAFOOD VEGETABLE DIP
EYE CATCHING, EASY, AND OH SO GOOD!

8 oz.	cream cheese	250 g
¼ cup	mayonnaise	60 mL
½ cup	sour cream	125 mL
2 x 4 oz.	cans of cocktail shrimp, drained	2 x 113 g
1 cup	seafood sauce	250 mL
2 cups	grated cheese (Cheddar and/OR mozzarella)	500 mL
1	green OR red pepper, chopped	1
1	tomato, seeded, diced	1
3	green onions, chopped a variety of crackers	3

- In a bowl, combine cream cheese, mayonnaise and sour cream until smooth. Spread evenly on a 12" (30 cm) round platter.
- Spread shrimp over cheese layer. Spread seafood sauce over shrimp. Sprinkle with cheeses and vegetables.
- Cover and chill until ready to serve. Serve with a variety of crackers.

YIELD   ***30 APPETIZER SERVINGS***

SHRIMP DIP

A COCKTAIL PARTY PLEASER

1 cup	sour cream	250 mL
8 oz.	cream cheese	250 g
2 tbsp.	onion soup mix (2 envelopes, 7 g)	30 mL
½ cup	chili sauce	125 mL
¼ cup	mayonnaise	60 mL
4 oz.	can shrimp, drained	113 g

- In a bowl combine the sour cream and cream cheese. Beat well.
- Add the onion soup mix, chili sauce and mayonnaise. Mix well.
- Add the shrimp and mix.
- Serve with a variety of vegetables and/or chips.

VARIATIONS   Crab, lobster, tuna or salmon can be substituted for the shrimp.

HINT   When using canned shrimp, improve its flavor by soaking the can in ice water for an hour before opening.

YIELD   *2 CUPS (500 ML)*

HOT SEAFOOD DIP

AN OUTSTANDING COMBINATION — HOT IN A CHAFING DISH OR
COLD THE NEXT DAY

8 oz.	cream cheese	250 g
1 cup	chopped crabmeat	250 mL
4 oz.	can shrimp, drained	113 g
1 tbsp.	horseradish	15 mL
1 tbsp.	lemon juice	15 mL
1 tbsp.	chili sauce	15 mL
3	green onions, chopped	3
1 cup	mayonnaise	250 mL

Hot seafood dip
(Continued)

- Combine all ingredients in a saucepan. Place over low heat stirring frequently until cheese melts.
- Serve hot along with cubed bread, crackers or a variety of dippers.

VARIATIONS   For a more intense cheese flavor, Velveeta cheese may be substituted for the cream cheese.

YIELD   **3 CUPS (750 ML)**

Crispy cheese appetizers
These crisp biscuits store well and are great with drinks

¾ cup	margarine	175 mL
8 oz.	Imperial sharp Cheddar cheese	250 g
1 cup	flour	250 mL
¼ tsp.	paprika	1 mL
3 cups	crisp rice cereal	750 mL

- In a large mixing bowl, cream together room temperature margarine and cheese.
- In another bowl, mix flour, paprika and rice cereal.
- Add flour mixture to cheese mixture. Mix until well blended.
- Drop dough mixture by tablespoons (15 mL portions) onto a lightly greased cookie sheet.
- Bake at 350°F (180°C) for about 10 minutes, or until crisp and golden.

VARIATION   Add a dash of cayenne pepper if you want a nippy flavor.

YIELD   **3½ DOZEN APPETIZERS**

BRUSCHETTA

A DELICIOUS APPETIZER OR ACCOMPANIMENT TO A SALAD OR SOUP

4	thick slices of Italian bread	4
2 tbsp.	olive oil	30 mL
1	small garlic clove, minced	1
1	large tomato, diced	1
1	green onion, chopped	1
2 tsp.	chopped fresh basil	10 mL
¼ tsp.	ground pepper	1 mL
2 oz.	grated mozzarella cheese	60 g

- Combine oil and garlic. Brush on bread slices.
- Combine tomato, onion, basil and pepper. Place on bread slices. Sprinkle cheese on top.
- Bake at 450°F (230°C) for about 5 minutes, or until hot.

VARIATION   For time-saving preparation and serving, especially for a large group, buy extra-chunky, extra-mild salsa and add crushed garlic, chopped fresh basil and oregano. Stir in olive oil and red wine vinegar to taste. Serve the Bruschetta topping in a bowl, surrounded by toasted baguette rounds. Guests can serve themselves.

YIELD   *4 SLICES*

CHILI CON QUESO

SERVE A BATCH WHEN WATCHING THE GAME OR A MOVIE

1	medium onion, chopped	1
1	green pepper, chopped	1
1	clove of garlic, minced	1
1 tbsp.	oil	15 mL
7 oz.	can diced green chilies	200 g
28 oz.	can whole tomatoes	796 mL
	jalapeño peppers, chopped (optional)	
1 lb.	Velveeta cheese, cubed	454 g

CHILI CON QUESO
(CONTINUED)

- In a heavy saucepan, sauté onion, pepper and garlic in oil for about 3 minutes, or until tender. Add green chilies, tomatoes and jalapeños. Simmer for 30 minutes, stirring occasionally, and breaking up tomatoes. Remove from heat. Cool slightly.
- Add the cheese. Return to low heat to allow cheese to melt. Mix well.
- Serve either warm or cold with tortilla chips.
- Refrigerate any extra for future use.

NOTE Whether jalapeños are added and the amount will depend on how spicy hot a flavor is preferred.

HINT If a cheese mixture becomes too hot and the cheese curdles, add 1 tsp. (5 mL) of baking soda and stir.

YIELD **6 CUPS (1.5 L)**

BLACK BEAN NACHOS
LOVELY TO LOOK AT, DELICIOUS TO EAT

1 lb.	nacho tortilla chips	454 g
19 oz.	can black beans	540 mL
½ cup	salsa	125 mL
1	small onion, finely chopped	1
2	garlic cloves , minced	2
1	green pepper, chopped	1
2	tomatoes, finely chopped	2
2 cups	grated Monterey Jack OR Cheddar cheese	500 mL

- Arrange nachos in a large roasting pan.
- In a saucepan, combine beans, salsa, onion, garlic and green pepper. Cook over medium heat until onion is tender. Remove from heat.
- Add tomatoes.
- Spoon bean mixture evenly over nachos. Top with cheese.
- Bake at 400°F (200°C) for 15 minutes, or until cheese is melted.

YIELD *12-16 APPETIZER SERVINGS*

See photograph on page 51.

SAUERKRAUT BITES

A TASTY, INTERESTING APPETIZER FOR THE SAUERKRAUT LOVER

1 lb.	ground pork	500 g
½ cup	chopped onion	125 mL
14 oz.	can sauerkraut, rinsed, well drained, chopped	398 mL
2 tbsp.	fine bread crumbs	30 mL
4 oz.	cream cheese	115 g
2 tbsp.	finely chopped fresh parsley	30 mL
1 tsp.	prepared mustard	5 mL
½ tsp.	garlic powder	2 mL
½ tsp.	pepper	2 mL
¼ cup	flour	60 mL
2	eggs, lightly beaten	2
¼ cup	milk	60 mL
¾ cup	fine bread crumbs	175 mL

- In a skillet over medium heat, cook pork until browned. Add onion and continue to cook until onion is translucent. Remove from heat. Drain off fat.
- To the onion, add the sauerkraut and bread crumbs. Combine well. Cool.
- Combine the cream cheese, parsley, mustard, garlic powder and pepper. Add to the pork mixture. Chill.
- When chilled, roll pork mixture into 1" (2.5 cm) balls, coat with flour and place on waxed paper.
- Combine the eggs and milk. Roll floured balls in egg mixture and then in bread crumbs.
- Place sauerkraut balls on a buttered cookie sheet. Bake, uncovered, at 400°F (200°C) for 15 minutes. Turn balls. Bake for an additional 15 minutes, or until hot and golden brown.

NOTE   These freeze well so they may be made in advance.

YIELD   **60 APPETIZERS**

APPETIZERS

Seafood-Stuffed Shells, page 44
Jalapeño Tortilla Rolls, page 44
Black Bean Nachos, page 49

SPINACH CHEESE PHYLLO PIE

No wonder the Greeks consider spanakopita one of their favorite appetizers. Try it!

2 lbs.	fresh spinach	1 kg
	salt	
½ cup	butter	125 mL
1 cup	chopped onion	250 mL
½ cup	chopped green onion	125 mL
½ cup	chopped fresh dill	125 mL
½ cup	chopped fresh parsley	125 mL
½ cup	half and half cream	125 mL
3	eggs	3
8 oz.	feta cheese, crumbled	250 g
½ cup	cottage cheese	125 mL
½ cup	butter, melted	125 mL
16 oz.	pkg. phyllo pastry leaves	454 g

- Wash spinach thoroughly. Chop. Sprinkle with salt. Spin in a vegetable drier until dry. Place in a bowl.
- In a large skillet in ½ cup (125 mL) butter, sauté both types of onion until translucent. Add dill, parsley and spinach. Cover. Cook until moisture has evaporated. Remove from heat. Add the cream.
- In a bowl, beat the eggs. Add the feta and cottage cheeses. Mix well and add to spinach mixture.
- Brush a 9 x 13" (23 x 33 cm) pan with some of the melted butter. Lay 8 phyllo leaves on the bottom of the pan, cutting away ends extending beyond the length of the pan. Spread spinach mixture over phyllo. Layer 8 more phyllo leaves on top. Brush with remaining melted butter. Score the top phyllo leaves into squares.
- Bake at 375°F (190°C) for 60 minutes, or until golden brown. Serve warm.

YIELD   *24 SQUARES*

PEPPERY CHEESE MELTS

THIS MAKE-AHEAD APPETIZER IS ALSO A GREAT BRIDGE CLUB TREAT

8 oz.	cream cheese	250 g
1 tbsp.	finely grated onion	15 mL
1 cup	mayonnaise	250 mL
½ tsp.	cayenne pepper	2 mL
½ cup	Parmesan cheese	125 mL
1	loaf of pumpernickel OR rye cocktail bread	1
	shrimp, pickles OR olives for garnish	

- In a bowl, mix the cream cheese, onion, mayonnaise, pepper and cheese.
- Spread each slice of bread with a generous portion of the cheese mixture. Place on a cookie sheet and place in freezer. When frozen, put in a container until ready to use.
- To serve, place bread slices on an ungreased cookie sheet. Bake at 350°F (180°C) for 10-15 minutes, or until cheese melts.
- Serve warm, garnished with cocktail shrimp, pickles or olives.

YIELD **20 APPETIZERS**

SHRIMP TARTS

GREAT FOR APPETIZERS OR FOR BRUNCH

24	unbaked tart shells, medium size	24
1	medium onion, chopped	1
3 tbsp.	butter	45 mL
3 tbsp.	flour	45 mL
1⅓ cups	milk	325 mL
2	egg yolks	2
1 tsp.	salt	5 mL
½ tsp.	pepper	2 mL
¾ cup	canned mushroom pieces	175 mL
4 oz.	can shrimp, drained	113 g

SHRIMP TARTS
(CONTINUED)

- Prepare the tart shells and set aside.
- In a skillet, sauté onions in butter. Sprinkle flour over and mix well. Add the milk and stir while bringing to a boil. Turn heat down; cook until thickened. Remove from heat.
- Add a little of the hot onion mixture to the egg yolks. Gradually stir the egg yolk mixture into the onion mixture. Beat well. Add the remaining ingredients. Divide evenly among the tart shells.
- Bake at 350°F (180°C) for 20 minutes, or until pastry is golden brown and filling is set.

YIELD *24 TARTS*

TARTS ALSACE
MEN ESPECIALLY LIKE THESE

24	unbaked tart shells, medium size	24
½ lb.	ground beef OR pork	250 g
⅓ cup	finely chopped onion	75 mL
1½ cups	shredded Swiss cheese	375 mL
4	eggs, lightly beaten	4
1½ cups	sour cream	375 mL
1 tsp.	salt	5 mL
½ tsp.	pepper	2 mL
1 tsp.	Worcestershire sauce	5 mL
	paprika	

- Prepare the tart shells and set aside.
- In a skillet over medium heat, cook meat until browned. Add onions and continue to cook until onions are translucent. Remove from heat. Drain off fat. Add cheese and mix well.
- Fill tart shells about half full with meat mixture.
- Combine eggs, sour cream, salt, pepper and Worcestershire sauce. Add 2 tbsp. (30 mL) of egg mixture to each tart shell. Sprinkle with paprika.
- Bake at 375°F (190°C) for 30 minutes, or until golden brown. Let sit for a few minutes. Serve warm.

YIELD *24 TARTS*

JUBILATION PUNCH

YOU'LL BE JUBILANT OVER HOW EASY THIS IS TO MAKE AND
HOW GOOD IT TASTES

14 oz.	can crushed pineapple	398 mL
10 oz.	can mandarin oranges	284 mL
12½ oz.	frozen pineapple juice concentrate	355 mL
26 oz.	vodka	750 mL
	ice	
2 x 2-qt.	bottles of ginger ale	2 x 2 L

- Combine the first 4 ingredients in a punch bowl.
- Add ice and ginger ale just before serving.

YIELD   *12-15 SERVINGS*

SUMMER SLUSH

SURE TO BE A HIT ON HOT SUMMER DAYS!

¾ cup	sugar	175 mL
1 cup	boiling water	250 mL
12 oz.	frozen lemonade concentrate	341 mL
12 oz.	frozen orange juice concentrate	341 mL
6 cups	hot water	1.5 L
26 oz.	vodka	750 mL
	ginger ale OR 7-Up	

- In a 4-quart (4 L) plastic pail, dissolve sugar in boiling water. Add the lemonade and orange juice concentrate. Mix well.
- Add the hot water. Mix well. Cool.
- Add the vodka.
- Put the lid on the pail and place in the freezer.
- To serve, fill a glass ⅓-½ full of frozen slush and top up with ginger ale.

YIELD   *20 SERVINGS*

CRANBERRY PUNCH

A REAL THIRST QUENCHER FOR A BACKYARD PICNIC

4 cups	cranberry juice	1 L
6 oz.	frozen lemonade concentrate	170 mL
8 cups	ginger ale	2 L

- Combine all ingredients in a punch bowl. Add ice cubes or an ice ring containing fruit (cherries, orange sections, raspberries, etc.).

YIELD   *12 CUPS (3 L)*

APPLE GRAPE PUNCH

A RE

CRANBERRY ORANGE PUNCH

GREAT ALL YEAR ROUND — FROM GARDEN PARTIES TO FESTIVE OCCASIONS

6 cups	cranberry juice	1.5 L
6 oz.	frozen orange juice concentrate	170 mL
3 tbsp.	lemon juice	45 mL
1¼ cups	pineapple juice	300 mL
3 cups	water	750 mL
	fresh fruit slices for garnish	

• Combine all ingredients in a punch bowl. Add ice cubes or an ice ring. Garnish with fresh fruit.

YIELD   *12 CUPS (3 L)*

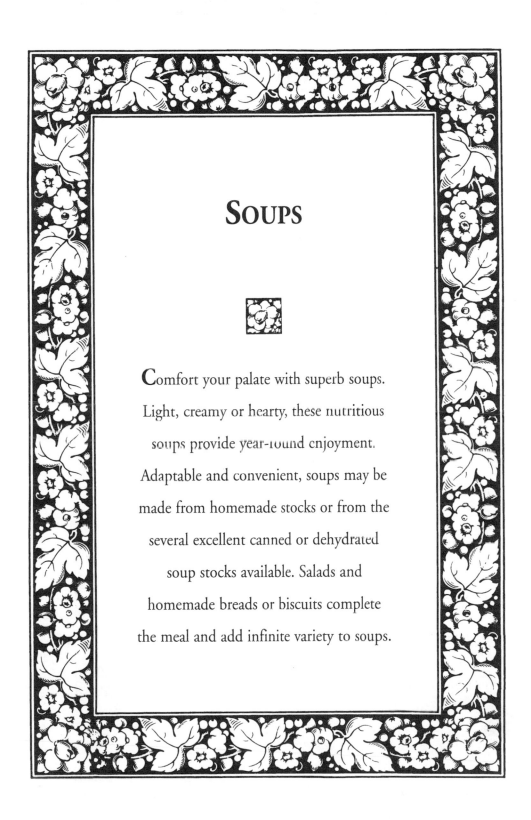

SOUPS

Comfort your palate with superb soups.
Light, creamy or hearty, these nutritious
soups provide year-round enjoyment.
Adaptable and convenient, soups may be
made from homemade stocks or from the
several excellent canned or dehydrated
soup stocks available. Salads and
homemade breads or biscuits complete
the meal and add infinite variety to soups.

CREAM OF LEEK SOUP

THIS VERSION OF THE CLASSIC VICHYSSOISE IS COMFORTING ON A CHILLY DAY

¼ cup	butter	60 mL
1 cup	sliced leeks (white part only)	250 mL
½ cup	chopped onion	125 mL
½ cup	chopped celery	125 mL
4 cups	water	1 L
1 tsp.	salt	5 mL
½ tsp.	pepper	2 mL
2 tbsp.	chopped fresh parsley	30 mL
1	bay leaf	1
2 cups	peeled and diced potatoes	500 mL
1 cup	milk	250 mL

- In a large saucepan, heat the butter and sauté leeks, onion and celery. Add water, salt, pepper, parsley and bay leaf. Simmer for 1 hour.
- Add potatoes and cook until tender.
- Add milk. Stir thoroughly. Heat but do not boil.
- Remove bay leaf. Serve hot.

VARIATION Chill soup and serve very cold, garnished with chopped chives or green onions.

YIELD *4 SERVINGS*

CAULIFLOWER SOUP

A LIGHT AND LOVELY SOUP OR APPETIZER

1 tbsp.	butter	15 mL
¼ cup	chopped onion	60 mL
2 cups	finely chopped cauliflower	500 mL
2 cups	chicken broth	500 mL
1 tsp.	dried tarragon	5 mL
1 tsp.	salt	5 mL
½ tsp.	pepper	2 mL
½ cup	milk	125 mL
1 tbsp.	flour	15 mL
¼ tsp.	nutmeg	1 mL

CAULIFLOWER SOUP

(CONTINUED)

- In a large, heavy saucepan, heat the butter and sauté the onion and cauliflower. Add the chicken broth, tarragon, salt and pepper. Let simmer until vegetables are tender.
- Combine the milk and flour, stirring until smooth. Add to the soup. Simmer until thoroughly heated.
- Sprinkle individual servings with nutmeg. Serve hot.

YIELD   **3-4 SERVINGS**

CREAM OF CELERY SOUP

SERVE WITH TOASTED SANDWICHES FOR A COOL-WEATHER SUPPER

1½ cups	chicken broth	375 mL
2 cups	chopped celery	500 mL
½ cup	chopped onion	125 mL
¼ tsp.	dried parsley	1 mL
¼ tsp.	dried tarragon	1 mL
2 tbsp.	butter	30 mL
2 tbsp.	flour	30 mL
¼ tsp.	salt	1 mL
¼ tsp.	pepper	1 mL
1 cup	milk	250 mL

- In a large saucepan, combine chicken broth, celery, onion, parsley and tarragon; cook until vegetables are tender.
- In a small saucepan, melt butter. Blend in flour, salt and pepper. Stir in the milk gradually. Cook and stir until mixture is thickened and bubbly. Add to the vegetable mixture. Stir until soup is thoroughly heated.

YIELD   **3-4 SERVINGS**

CORN-BACON CHOWDER

A GREAT STARTER AFTER A DAY ON THE SLOPES

2	slices bacon, chopped	2
1	medium onion, finely chopped	1
2 tbsp.	flour	30 mL
1 cup	milk	250 mL
1 tsp.	salt	5 mL
½ tsp.	Worcestershire sauce	2 mL
2 cups	milk	500 mL
14 oz.	can cream-style corn	398 mL

- In a skillet, fry bacon until crisp. Remove bacon from skillet.
- In bacon fat in skillet, sauté onion until tender.
- To onion in skillet, add flour, 1 cup (250 mL) of milk, salt and Worcestershire sauce. Cook slowly until thickened. Transfer to a 2-quart (2 L) saucepan.
- To saucepan, add remaining milk, corn and bacon pieces. Bring to a boil, stirring constantly. Cook for 2 minutes. Serve.

VARIATIONS If you like a touch of heat or a lot of heat in your food, add 3-4 drops of your favorite hot pepper sauce and/or some finely chopped jalapeño pepper.

YIELD **4-5 SERVINGS**

CORN 'N' SAUSAGE CHOWDER

A QUICK BUT VERY TASTY CHOWDER FOR BUSY WINTER DAYS!

½ lb.	sausage links	250 g
12 oz.	can whole kernel corn, undrained	341 mL
14 oz.	can cream-style corn	398 mL
10 oz.	can cream of celery soup	284 mL
1½ cups	milk	375 mL

CORN 'N' SAUSAGE CHOWDER
(CONTINUED)

- In a skillet, fry sausage links until fully cooked. Cut into ½" (1 cm) pieces.
- In a saucepan, over medium heat, combine sausage pieces and remaining ingredients. Stir frequently until thoroughly heated.

VARIATIONS   Try pure pork or pork and beef sausages. You can also use spicy Italian or Spanish (Chorizo) sausages.

YIELD   **5 SERVINGS**

CABBAGE SOUP
FOR A FULL MEAL, SERVE WITH A CORNED BEEF ON RYE SANDWICH

1 tbsp.	cooking oil	15 mL
½ lb.	lean boneless pork, cubed	250 g
1	medium onion, chopped	1
2	garlic cloves, minced	2
2	celery stalks, chopped	2
2½ cups	beef broth	625 mL
14 oz.	can tomato sauce	398 mL
1	small cabbage, shredded	1
1	bay leaf	1
½ tsp.	salt	2 mL
¼ tsp.	pepper	1 mL
½ tsp.	paprika	2 mL
	sour cream (optional)	

- In a Dutch oven, heat cooking oil and brown the pork. Add onion, garlic and celery. Cook until vegetables are just tender.
- Add beef broth to pork, along with remaining ingredients, except sour cream. Bring the soup to a boil.
- Reduce heat, simmer and continue to cook for 1 hour, or until meat is tender. Remove bay leaf.
- Serve garnished with a dollop of sour cream, if desired.

YIELD   **5-6 SERVINGS**

TACO SOUP

A COUSIN TO CHILI CON CARNE — AND EVERY BIT AS DELICIOUS

1 lb.	lean ground beef	500 g
1	medium onion, chopped	1
2	garlic cloves, minced	2
1 tbsp.	taco seasoning (see recipe below)	15 mL
19 oz.	can kidney beans, undrained	540 mL
12 oz.	can kernel corn, undrained	341 mL
28 oz.	can stewed tomatoes	796 mL
1	green pepper, chopped (optional)	1
5½ oz.	can tomato paste	156 mL
	water	
	sour cream	
	grated Cheddar cheese	
	tortilla chips	

- In a Dutch oven, brown ground beef. Add onion and garlic and cook until onions are translucent.
- Add taco seasoning, beans, corn, tomatoes, green pepper and tomato paste. Simmer slowly, stirring occasionally, for 2 hours.
- Add water to obtain desired consistency.
- Serve garnished with sour cream and Cheddar cheese. Tortilla chips can be served on the side or crumbled into the soup.

YIELD   5-6 SERVINGS

See photograph on page 69.

TACO SEASONING MIX

½ cup	salt	125 mL
½ cup	chili powder	125 mL
¼ cup	crushed, dried red chili peppers	60 mL
¼ cup	instant minced garlic	60 mL
2 tbsp.	ground oregano	30 mL
¼ cup	cumin	60 mL

- Combine all ingredients. Store in a cool place. Use as required.

HAMBURGER SOUP

ITS LASTING POPULARITY SPEAKS FOR ITSELF

1 tbsp.	vegetable oil	15 mL
1 lb.	ground lean beef	500 g
1	medium onion, chopped	1
4 cups	beef broth	1 L
28 oz.	can tomatoes	796 mL
4	potatoes, peeled and diced	4
4	carrots, chopped	4
3	celery stalks, chopped	3
1 cup	shredded cabbage	250 mL
14 oz.	can tomato sauce	398 mL
1	bay leaf	1
¼ tsp.	thyme	1 mL
¼ tsp.	basil	1 mL
1 tsp.	salt	5 mL
½ tsp.	pepper	2 mL

- In a skillet, heat oil and brown the beef. Add the onions and continue to sauté until onions are translucent. Transfer to a Dutch oven or a slow cooker.
- Add beef broth to the beef mixture.
- Add remaining ingredients. Cover and cook slowly for 3-4 hours, or until vegetables are tender.
- If desired, extra liquid may be added to obtain desired consistency.

VARIATION To extend this soup or to vary it, add ½-1 cup (125-250 mL) of small pasta shells or noodles.

YIELD **6-8 SERVINGS**

Manhattan Clam Chowder

A PLEASING ALTERNATIVE TO BOSTON CLAM CHOWDER

4	bacon slices, chopped	4
1	large onion, chopped	1
½ cup	chopped celery	125 mL
2 cups	water	500 mL
2 cups	peeled and diced potatoes	500 mL
2 tsp.	salt	10 mL
½ tsp.	pepper	2 mL
28 oz.	can tomatoes	796 mL
1	bay leaf	1
2 x 10 oz.	cans of clams	2 x 284 mL

- In a large heavy saucepan, cook bacon. Add onions and celery. Cook until onions are translucent.
- Add remaining ingredients, except for clams. Simmer gently for 1-2 hours, or until vegetables are tender. Add clams for the last 10 minutes of cooking. Remove bay leaf. Serve hot.

VARIATIONS Add a few drops of hot pepper sauce or use herb and spice or Mexican-flavored canned tomatoes instead of the regular canned tomatoes.

YIELD **5 SERVINGS**

Pizza Soup

GUARANTEED TO BE A HIT WITH THE YOUNG CROWD

1 tbsp.	vegetable oil	15 mL
2	garlic cloves, minced	2
1	medium onion, chopped	1
½	green pepper, chopped	½
1 cup	sliced fresh mushrooms	250 mL
28 oz.	can tomatoes, undrained	796 mL
8 oz.	pepperoni, thinly sliced	250 g
3 cups	beef broth	750 mL
½ tsp.	dried basil	2 mL
⅔ cup	dry elbow macaroni	150 mL
	salt and pepper to taste	
	shredded mozzarella cheese	

PIZZA SOUP
(CONTINUED)

- In a large saucepan, heat oil and sauté the garlic, onions, pepper and mushrooms until vegetables are tender, about 5 minutes.
- Add tomatoes, pepperoni, beef broth, basil and macaroni. Bring to a boil, reduce heat and continue to simmer until macaroni is tender, about 40 minutes. Season with salt and pepper to taste.
- Serve soup with cheese sprinkled on the top.

YIELD   6 SERVINGS

MINESTRONE

SERVE WITH A CRUSTY ROLL AND A PIECE OF CHEESE, AND DINNER IS COMPLETE

2 tbsp.	butter	30 mL
1	medium onion, chopped	1
2	celery stalks, chopped	2
4 cups	chicken broth	1 L
2	carrots, finely chopped	2
1	bay leaf	1
½ tsp.	ground oregano	2 mL
½ tsp.	garlic powder	2 mL
½ tsp.	salt	2 mL
½ tsp.	pepper	2 mL
28 oz.	can tomatoes	796 mL
⅔ cup	uncooked shell pasta	150 mL
	Parmesan cheese	

- In a skillet, heat butter and sauté onion and celery until soft. Transfer to a large soup pot.
- Add remaining ingredients, except Parmesan cheese. Heat to boiling. Reduce heat. Simmer until vegetables and pasta are well cooked, about 40 minutes.
- Remove bay leaf. Serve hot. Sprinkle with Parmesan cheese, if desired.

YIELD   6 SERVINGS

BLACK BEAN SOUP

A THICK HEARTY SOUP WHICH IS QUICKLY GAINING POPULARITY

1 cup	dry black beans	250 mL
5 cups	water	1.25 L
4	bacon slices, chopped	4
1	small onion, chopped	1
1	carrot, chopped	1
1	celery stalk, chopped	1
2	garlic cloves, minced	2
1	green pepper, chopped	1
½ cup	chili sauce	125 mL
1	bay leaf	1
½ tsp.	ground cumin	2 mL
1½ tsp.	salt	7 mL
½ tsp.	black pepper	2 mL
½ tsp.	cayenne pepper	2 mL
1½ tsp.	vinegar	7 mL
2 tbsp.	chopped pimiento	30 mL
2 tbsp.	sherry	30 mL
	chicken broth	
	chopped green onion	
	chopped boiled egg	

- Soak beans in water overnight. Drain. In a large saucepan, cover beans with fresh water and cook for 1½-2 hours, or until tender.
- In a skillet over medium heat, cook bacon with onion, carrot, celery, garlic and green pepper, until vegetables begin to soften. Add to beans.
- Add chili sauce, bay leaf, cumin, salt, black pepper and cayenne pepper. Cover and simmer for 2-3 hours.
- Add vinegar, pimiento and sherry. Cook for 30 minutes more to blend flavors. Remove bay leaf. Mash beans slightly.
- If necessary, add chicken broth for desired consistency.
- Serve garnished with chopped green onion and chopped egg.

VARIATION   Try a dollop of sour cream for garnish. Also try chopped tomatoes, green peppers, onions and grated Cheddar cheese as garnishes.

YIELD   *4-6 SERVINGS*

SOUP AND BREAD

Taco Soup, page 64
Whole-Wheat Soda Bread, page 17

ORIENTAL HOT AND SOUR SOUP

AN INTERESTING BLEND OF FLAVORS WITH LOTS OF VEGGIES

1 tbsp.	sesame oil	15 mL
3	garlic cloves, minced	3
6 cups	chicken broth	1.5 L
⅓ cup	red wine vinegar	75 mL
1 tbsp.	soy sauce	15 mL
2 tsp.	hot pepper sauce	10 mL
1 tsp.	Worcestershire sauce	5 mL
½ tsp.	pepper	2 mL
1 cup	chopped cooked chicken, pork OR beef	250 mL
10½ oz.	pkg. firm tofu, cubed	297 g
1	carrot, cut into julienne strips	1
8	fresh mushrooms, sliced	8
3	green onions, cut into julienne strips	3
½ cup	bean sprouts	125 mL
3	leaves bok choy (Chinese cabbage), cut into julienne strips	3
12-15	fresh snow peas	12-15

- In a large saucepan or a Dutch oven, heat sesame oil and sauté garlic. Add remaining ingredients, except bok choy and snow peas. Bring to a boil, reduce heat to a simmer and cook until carrots are tender, about 30 minutes.
- Add bok choy and peas. Cook until vegetables are just tender, about 5 minutes.

VARIATIONS   A small can of flaked chicken can be substituted for the cooked meat. Beef broth can be substituted for the chicken broth.

YIELD   *6 SERVINGS*

MIRACLE SOUP

A GREAT SOUP FOR THE DIETER!

1½ oz.	onion soup mix (1 envelope)	40 g
4 cups	water	1 L
2	carrots, finely chopped	2
2	celery stalks, chopped	2
½	green pepper, chopped	½
1 tbsp.	finely chopped parsley	15 mL
1 cup	chopped mushrooms	250 mL
1 cup	chopped broccoli	250 mL
1 cup	chopped spinach	250 mL
1	garlic clove, minced	1
½ tsp.	allspice	2 mL
½ tsp.	paprika	2 mL
1 tsp.	salt	5 mL
½ tsp.	pepper	2 mL

- In a saucepan, combine the onion soup mix and water. Bring to a boil. Add remaining ingredients. Simmer for 2-3 hours.

YIELD   **3-4 SERVINGS**

SALADS, DRESSINGS, SAUCES & CONDIMENTS

Relish the refreshing flavor of great
salads. Green salads with crisp leafy
lettuces, vegetable, fruit and meat salads,
tart marinated vegetable salads, sparkling
jellied salads enhance soup or main course
meals. Main course salads create inviting
lunches and light suppers served with
crusty breads and rolls.

MELON AND CHICKEN SALAD

A GREAT CHOICE FOR A LADIES' LUNCHEON

LEMON YOGURT DRESSING:

½ cup	plain yogurt	125 mL
⅓ cup	mayonnaise	75 mL
3 tbsp.	lemon juice	45 mL
½ tsp.	salt	2 mL
½ tsp.	pepper	2 mL
2 cups	diced cooked chicken	500 mL
1 cup	diced cantaloupe melon	250 mL
1 cup	diced honeydew melon	250 mL
½ cup	chopped celery	125 mL
2	green onions, chopped	2
	a variety of lettuce leaves	
	kale (optional)	
½ cup	cashews (optional)	125 mL
	blueberries	
	paprika	

- In a small bowl, combine the dressing ingredients.
- Combine the chicken, melon, celery and onions.
- Add enough of the dressing to just coat the chicken mixture. Refrigerate for an hour before serving.
- Serve salad on greens. Garnish with cashews, blueberries and paprika.

NOTE The yogurt dressing may be used on other fruit salads or as a fruit dip. Omit the salt and pepper and add 1 tbsp. (15 mL) of honey.

YIELD *4 SERVINGS/1 CUP (250 ML) OF DRESSING*

See photograph on page 87.

SPINACH WALDORF SALAD

TRY VARIOUS FRUITS TO FIT THE SEASON

POPPY SEED DRESSING:

½ cup	sugar	125 mL
1 tsp.	dry mustard	5 mL
1 tsp.	salt	5 mL
⅓ cup	vinegar	75 mL
½	medium onion, finely chopped	½
1 cup	vegetable oil	250 mL
2 tbsp.	poppy seeds	30 mL

6 cups	fresh spinach, rinsed	1.5 L
2 tbsp.	lemon juice	30 mL
1	red apple	1
1	yellow OR green apple	1
2	celery stalks, chopped	2
¼ cup	raisins	60 mL
½ cup	grapes	125 mL
¼ cup	pecan pieces (optional)	60 mL

- In a blender, combine sugar, mustard, salt, vinegar and onion. Add oil slowly while blending. Add poppy seeds and continue to beat until thick and well blended.
- Tear spinach into bite-sized pieces and place in a salad bowl.
- Pour lemon juice into a small bowl. Core and cube apples and place in lemon juice. Stir to coat apple pieces to prevent discoloring. Drain off extra juice. Add celery, raisins and grapes to apples. Add enough poppy seed dressing to thoroughly coat fruit.
- When ready to serve, mix fruit in with spinach. Toss. Add pecans if desired. Serve with additional dressing on the side.

YIELD   *6 SERVINGS/2 CUPS (500 ML) OF DRESSING*

See photograph on the front cover.

SPINACH FRUIT SALAD

LIGHT AND LOVELY FOR SULTRY SUMMER DAYS

8 oz.	fresh spinach	250 g
⅓ cup	mayonnaise	75 mL
1 tbsp.	lemon juice	15 mL
¼ tsp.	ground ginger	1 mL
3	pears, cubed	3
10 oz.	can mandarin oranges, drained	284 mL
⅓ cup	seedless raisins	75 mL
⅓ cup	sunflower seeds	75 mL

- Wash and tear spinach into bite-sized pieces.
- In a bowl, combine mayonnaise, lemon juice and ginger.
- To mayonnaise add remaining ingredients. Toss and serve over spinach.

YIELD   *4-6 SERVINGS*

SALAD OF THE GODS

EXTRA SPECIAL — JUST LIKE ITS NAME

TARRAGON LEMON DRESSING:

½ cup	white wine vinegar	125 mL
¼ cup	vegetable oil	60 mL
1 tbsp.	lemon juice	15 mL
½ tsp.	ground tarragon	2 mL
¼ tsp.	ground marjoram	1 mL
¼ tsp.	salt	1 mL
¼ tsp.	sugar	1 mL
¼ tsp.	pepper	1 mL
1	head romaine lettuce	1
19 oz.	can pineapple chunks	540 mL
20 oz.	can lychees in syrup (optional)	565 g
1	red apple	1
1	orange, peeled and sliced	1
½ lb.	seedless red OR green grapes	250 g

SALAD OF THE GODS
(CONTINUED)

- At least a day in advance, combine dressing ingredients in a blender. Blend, place in a jar and refrigerate until ready to use.
- Next day, wash lettuce and tear into bite-sized pieces.
- Drain pineapple, reserving liquid. Drain lychees thoroughly.
- Core apple and chop coarsely. Immerse in reserved pineapple juice to prevent discoloring. Prepare orange. Halve grapes.
- Combine pineapple chunks, lychees, drained apple pieces, orange slices and grapes. Toss lightly with some of the dressing.
- Combine the fruit with the lettuce. Toss lightly. Serve with additional dressing on the side.

YIELD   *6 SERVINGS*

See photograph on page 33.

TABBOULEH
A MIDDLE EASTERN DISH WHICH IS DESERVING OF ITS POPULARITY!

⅔ cup	bulgur (crushed wheat)	150 mL
2 cups	chopped fresh parsley	500 mL
2 tbsp.	chopped fresh mint	30 mL
2	green onions, chopped	2
1	yellow pepper, chopped (optional)	1
¼ cup	olive oil	60 mL
2 tbsp.	lemon juice	30 mL
2	garlic cloves, crushed	2
1	large tomato, chopped and seeded	1
	romaine lettuce leaves	

- Place bulgur in a mixing bowl. Cover with hot water. Set aside for 30 minutes. Drain and squeeze dry.
- Combine bulgur with remaining ingredients, except tomatoes and lettuce leaves. Cover. Refrigerate for 2 hours, stirring occasionally.
- Just before serving add tomatoes. Toss well.
- To eat, tear lettuce into bite-sized pieces and use to scoop up tabbouleh.

YIELD   *12 APPETIZER OR 4 MAIN COURSE SERVINGS*

CAESAR SALAD

A CLASSIC SALAD THAT IS STILL A FAVORITE

CAESAR DRESSING:

½ cup	olive oil	125 mL
2 tbsp.	lemon juice	30 mL
1 tsp.	red wine vinegar	5 mL
2	garlic cloves	2
1 tsp.	prepared mustard	5 mL
½ tsp.	Worcestershire sauce	2 mL
1	egg	1
4	capers (optional)	4
2 tsp.	anchovy paste (optional)	10 mL
¼ tsp.	salt	1 mL
¼ tsp.	freshly ground pepper	1 mL
1	head Romaine lettuce	1
½ cup	grated Parmesan cheese	125 mL
½ cup	crumbled crisp bacon	125 mL
1 cup	croûtons	250 mL

- Combine dressing ingredients in a blender. Blend. Refrigerate until ready to use.
- Tear lettuce into bite-sized pieces. Sprinkle with half of the Parmesan cheese and toss well. Pour some of the dressing over and again toss well. Top with bacon bits and croûtons.
- Serve salad with remaining dressing and cheese on the side.

YIELD   8 SERVINGS

GREEK SALAD

FRESH, COLORFUL, DELECTABLE!

2	large tomatoes, seeded, cut into wedges	2
1	English cucumber, unpeeled, cut into thick slices	1
1	green pepper, cut into 1" (2 cm) chunks	1
1	sweet white onion, sliced	1
2	celery stalks, cut into ½" (1.3 cm) diagonal chunks	2
4 oz.	feta cheese, crumbled	115 g
4 oz.	Calamata olives	115 g

GREEK SALAD DRESSING:

½ cup	olive oil	125 mL
2 tbsp.	lemon juice	30 mL
2 tbsp.	red wine vinegar	30 mL
1	garlic clove, minced	1
½ tsp.	dried oregano	2 mL

- Place salad ingredients in a bowl.
- In a blender, combine dressing ingredients.
- To serve, toss dressing over vegetables to coat lightly.
- Pass additional dressing with salad.

YIELD   *6 SERVINGS*

MARINATED ONIONS

A POPULAR SIDE DISH TO ACCOMPANY A BEEF BARBECUE!

4	large onions	4
1 cup	vinegar	250 mL
½ cup	white sugar	125 mL
¼ cup	mayonnaise	60 mL
1 tsp.	celery seed	5 mL

- Peel and slice onions. Divide into rings. Place in a glass bowl.
- In a saucepan, mix vinegar and sugar. Bring to a boil. Pour over the onions. Refrigerate for a minimum of 6 hours. Drain.
- To serve, combine mayonnaise and celery seed with onions.

YIELD   ***8-10 SERVINGS***

TOMATO MOZZARELLA SALAD

THIS VERY SIMPLE SALAD IS WONDERFUL WITH FRESH GARDEN TOMATOES —
ITALIAN GRANDMOTHERS HAVE BEEN MAKING IT FOR GENERATIONS!

6	ripe tomatoes, thickly sliced	6
1¼ lbs.	mozzarella cheese, thickly sliced	625 g
8-10	fresh basil leaves, coarsely chopped	8-10
	red wine vinegar (optional)	
¼ cup	extra virgin olive oil, OR more, to taste	60 mL
	salt and freshly ground pepper to taste	

- On a large serving plate or in a shallow bowl, alternate tomato and mozzarella slices. Sprinkle with coarsely chopped basil and drizzle with vinegar and olive oil. Serve at once.

NOTE   Mozzarella should be sliced about half as thick as tomatoes.

VARIATIONS Substitute fresh bocconcini, a mild unripened Italian cheese, for the mozzarella. Substitute 2 tbsp. (30 mL) of chopped fresh oregano for the basil or use it in addition to the basil. Sprinkle 2-3 tbsp. (30-45 mL) of capers over the salad. You can even omit the cheese entirely and enjoy the fresh tomatoes with basil, vinegar and oil or add thinly sliced sweet onions instead of the cheese.

YIELD   ***6-8 SERVINGS***

BROCCOLI SALAD

INDIFFERENT TO BROCCOLI? THIS YOU WILL ENJOY!

1	large bunch broccoli	1
12	bacon slices	12
1	medium red onion, chopped	1
2 cups	grated Cheddar cheese	500 mL

DRESSING:

½ cup	mayonnaise-type salad dressing	125 mL
2 tbsp.	sugar	30 mL
1 tbsp.	vinegar	15 mL

- Wash broccoli, peel stems and chop stems and florets into small pieces.
- Fry bacon until crisp. Break into small pieces.
- In a large mixing bowl combine broccoli, bacon, onion and cheese.
- Combine dressing ingredients. Toss vegetables with dressing. Serve.

VARIATIONS   Omit cheese and add 1 cup (250 mL) raisins and 1 cup (250 mL) raw sunflower seeds. Add 2 tbsp. (30 mL) Honey Mustard Sauce, page 94, to the dressing. Omit red onion and add 3 green onions, chopped.

YIELD   *8-10 SERVINGS*

TACO SALAD

A TASTY MEAL-IN-ONE SALAD

1 lb.	lean ground beef	500 g
1	head lettuce	1
1 lb.	Cheddar cheese, grated	500 g
2	green onions, chopped	2
2	celery stalks, chopped	2
12	ripe olives, sliced	12
2	tomatoes, cubed	2
8 oz.	bottle of green onion dressing	250 mL
¼ cup	taco seasoning mix*	60 mL
8 oz.	bag taco-flavored tortilla chips, crushed	240 g

- In a skillet, sauté beef until well-browned. Drain off fat.
- Tear lettuce into bite-sized pieces.
- In a large mixing bowl, combine beef, lettuce, cheese, onions, celery, olives and tomatoes.
- In a small bowl, combine green onion dressing and taco seasoning mix. Add to beef and vegetables and toss until well mixed.
- When ready to serve add tortilla chips. Mix lightly and serve.

* Use the taco seasoning mix on page 64 or buy a commercial mix.

YIELD   *6 SERVINGS*

MACARONI AND SALMON SALAD

AN ADAPTABLE OLD FAMILY FAVORITE

4 cups	cooked elbow macaroni	1 L
4	hard-boiled eggs, peeled and chopped	4
3	green onions, chopped	3
1 cup	chopped celery	250 mL
½ cup	diced cucumber	125 mL
5 oz.	can sockeye salmon, drained	142 g
1 tsp.	salt	5 mL
½ tsp.	pepper	2 mL
½ cup	mayonnaise	125 mL
½ tsp.	paprika	2 mL

MACARONI AND SALMON SALAD

(CONTINUED)

- In a large bowl, combine macaroni, eggs, vegetables and salmon.
- Combine salt, pepper and mayonnaise. Mix with macaroni mixture. Sprinkle paprika on top.
- Refrigerate until ready to serve.

VARIATION Substitute 1½ cups (375 mL) of cubed cooked ham for salmon. Add 1 tsp. (5 mL) of prepared mustard to mayonnaise dressing.

YIELD *6-8 SERVINGS*

SPAGHETTI SALAD

8 oz.	uncooked spaghetti	250 g
16 oz.	bottle of Italian dressing	500 mL
2	cucumbers, peeled and diced	2
2	tomatoes, diced	2
1	small red onion, chopped	1
1	green pepper, chopped	1
2 tbsp.	grated Parmesan cheese	30 mL
1 tbsp.	poppy seeds	15 mL
1 tbsp.	sesame seed (optional)	15 mL
1 tbsp.	celery seed (optional)	15 mL
½ tsp.	salt	2 mL
½ tsp.	pepper	2 mL

- Break spaghetti lengths into fourths. Cook according to package directions. Drain and cool. Marinate overnight in Italian dressing.
- Add remaining ingredients. Mix well.
- Refrigerate until ready to serve.

YIELD *8 SERVINGS*

JAPANESE NOODLES COLESLAW

AN INTERESTING BLEND OF FLAVORS AND TEXTURES

1	small cabbage, shredded	1
6	green onions, chopped	6
½ cup	slivered almonds	125 mL
½ cup	raw sunflower seeds	125 mL
¼ cup	vegetable oil	60 mL
¼ cup	vinegar	60 mL
3½ oz.	pkg. Ichiban noodles, original flavor mix	100 g

- In a large bowl, combine cabbage and onions.
- In a skillet, brown almonds and sunflower seeds. Set aside.
- In a small bowl, combine vegetable oil, vinegar and seasoning package from noodles. Toss with vegetables. This can be done up to a day in advance of serving.
- Just prior to serving, crush Ichiban noodles. Add noodles, almonds and sunflower seeds to cabbage. Toss to mix. Serve at once.

YIELD   *8-10 SERVINGS*

SAUERKRAUT SALAD

A LONG-TIME FAVORITE THAT IS GOOD FOR A BUFFET!

14 oz.	can sauerkraut	398 mL
3	green onions, chopped	3
1	green pepper, chopped	1
1	carrot, grated	1
½ cup	sugar	125 mL
1 tsp.	celery salt	5 mL

SAUERKRAUT SALAD
(CONTINUED)

- Prepare salad at least 12 hours before serving.
- Rinse and drain sauerkraut thoroughly.
- In a glass bowl, mix sauerkraut with vegetables.
- Sprinkle sugar and celery salt over sauerkraut mixture.
- Cover and refrigerate.
- Mix thoroughly before serving.

YIELD   **6-8 SERVINGS**

WHEAT SALAD
GREAT AS A SALAD OR DESSERT

2 cups	raw wheat	500 mL
8 oz.	cream cheese	250 g
14 oz.	can crushed pineapple	398 mL
2 x 4 oz.	pkgs. vanilla instant pudding	2 x 113 g
3 tbsp.	lemon juice	45 mL
1½ cups	chopped walnuts (optional)	375 mL
4 cups	whipped topping	1 L

- Place wheat in a saucepan. Cover with water. Soak overnight.
- The next day, bring wheat in water to a gentle boil. Cook slowly for 2 hours, or until wheat is tender. Drain and cool.
- In a mixing bowl combine cheese, pineapple, instant puddings, lemon juice and walnuts. Mix well.
- Add the cooked wheat. Fold in whipped topping. Chill.

NOTE   This recipe is easily halved with favorable results. Any leftovers refrigerate well for 2-3 days.

VARIATIONS   2 cups (500 mL) of mashed cottage cheese can be substituted for the cream cheese. For an interesting variation, substitute pistachio instant pudding for the vanilla instant pudding.

YIELD   **8-10 SERVINGS**

TOMATO ASPIC

SPICY AND COLORFUL!

5 tsp.	unflavored gelatin	25 mL
¼ cup	cold water	60 mL
2 cups	tomato juice	500 mL
1 tsp.	sugar	5 mL
2 tbsp.	lemon juice	30 mL
¼ tsp.	garlic powder	1 mL
¼ tsp.	paprika	1 mL
¼ tsp.	cayenne pepper	1 mL
¼ tsp.	celery salt	1 mL
¾ cup	grated carrots	175 mL
¼ cup	chopped ripe olives (optional)	60 mL
½ cup	chopped celery	125 mL
2	green onions, chopped	2

- Soak gelatin in cold water.
- In a saucepan, combine tomato juice, sugar, lemon juice and spices. Bring to a boil. Remove from heat.
- Add gelatin mixture. Blend well.
- Chill. When juice begins to thicken add vegetables.
- Pour into a jelly mold. Chill.
- To serve, unmold and garnish.

YIELD   6 SERVINGS

SALAD AND BREAD

CUCUMBER JELLIED SALAD

LIGHT AND REFRESHING FOR A SUMMER DAY

6 oz.	pkg. lemon gelatin	170 g
1 cup	boiling water	250 mL
1 tbsp.	vinegar	15 mL
1	medium cucumber, chopped	1
1	medium onion, chopped	1
1 cup	small-curd cottage cheese	250 mL
1 cup	mayonnaise-type salad dressing	250 mL
½ cup	chopped walnuts	60 mL

- Dissolve gelatin in boiling water. Add vinegar. Stir until well mixed.
- Chill until partially set. Add remaining ingredients. Mix well.
- Pour into a serving dish or mold. Chill until firm.

YIELD   *6-8 SERVINGS*

JELLIED RICE SALAD

AN INTERESTING ADDITION TO A BUFFET

3 oz.	pkg. gelatin (any flavor)	85 g
1 cup	boiling water	250 mL
14 oz.	can pineapple tidbits, drained, juice reserved	398 mL
1 cup	cooked rice	250 mL
8 oz.	pkg. minimarshmallows	250 g
1 tsp.	lemon juice	5 mL
1	apple, chopped	1
1 cup	whipping cream, whipped	250 mL

- In a mixing bowl, dissolve gelatin in boiling water. Add pineapple juice and enough water to make 1 cup (250 mL). Chill until partially set.
- Combine rice, marshmallows, lemon juice, apple and pineapple tidbits. Fold into gelatin mixture.
- Fold whipped cream into gelatin mixture. Chill.

YIELD   *6-8 SERVINGS*

YOGURT HERB DRESSING

A MULTI-PURPOSE FLAVORFUL BLEND

½ cup	plain yogurt	125 mL
½ cup	mayonnaise	125 mL
¼ cup	milk	60 mL
½ tsp.	sugar	2 mL
½ tsp.	salt	2 mL
¼ tsp.	dried oregano	1 mL
¼ tsp.	dried dillweed	1 mL
¼ tsp.	dried basil	1 mL

- Combine all of the ingredients. Blend well. Chill.
- Serve on tossed green salads or as a topping for baked potatoes.

YIELD   *1 CUP (250 ML)*

COOKED SALAD DRESSING

OLD-FASHIONED COOKED MAYONNAISE-TYPE DRESSING WITH A ZING!

1 tsp.	salt	5 mL
2 tsp.	dry mustard	10 mL
1 cup	sugar	250 mL
1 tsp.	paprika	5 mL
½ tsp.	pepper	2 mL
2 tbsp.	flour	30 mL
2	eggs, beaten	2
1 cup	vinegar	250 mL
1 cup	milk, scalded	250 mL
1 tsp.	butter	5 mL

Cooked Salad Dressing
(Continued)

- In a saucepan, combine dry ingredients.
- Combine eggs with vinegar. Add to dry ingredients. Mix well.
- Add scalded milk. Bring to a boil. Reduce heat and cook for 10-12 minutes, or until thickened and smooth.
- Add butter. Continue to cook for an additional 2 minutes.

SERVING SUGGESTIONS Use on macaroni and potato salads. To use on green salads, thin with cream. This is an excellent accompaniment to cold cuts.

YIELD **2 CUPS (500 ML)**

Lemon Dill Sauce
Excellent with barbecued salmon!

1 tbsp.	butter	15 mL
1 tbsp.	flour	15 mL
¾ cup	milk	175 mL
¼ cup	mayonnaise	60 mL
1 tbsp.	snipped fresh dill	15 mL
1 tbsp.	grated lemon rind	15 ml
	salt and pepper to taste	

- In a saucepan, melt butter. Add flour. Combine well. Add the milk. Blend together with a whisk. Cook until mixture thickens. Remove from heat.
- Stir in mayonnaise, dill and lemon rind. Add salt and pepper, if desired.

YIELD **1 CUP (250 ML)**

GARLIC BUTTER

GREAT TO HAVE ON HAND — GOOD FOR BUNS OR BREAD!

1 lb.	butter OR margarine	500 g
1	head of garlic, cloves peeled, crushed	1
1 tsp.	lemon juice	5 mL
3	drops Worcestershire sauce	3
3	drops Tabasco sauce	3
2 tbsp.	grated Parmesan cheese	30 mL
1 tsp.	dried parsley flakes	5 mL
	salt and pepper to taste	

• In a mixing bowl, combine all ingredients, except salt and pepper. Mix well. Add salt and pepper to taste as desired. Store in a covered container in the refrigerator and use as needed.

YIELD   2 CUPS (500 ML)

TARTAR SAUCE

MAKES THE CATCH OF THE DAY EXTRAORDINAIRE

1 cup	mayonnaise	250 mL
2 tbsp.	finely chopped dill pickle	30 mL
2 tbsp.	finely chopped onion	30 mL
2 tbsp.	finely chopped olives	30 mL
2 tsp.	lemon juice	10 mL
	pinch of pepper	

• Combine ingredients well. Place in a covered container. Refrigerate until ready to use.

YIELD   2 CUPS (500 ML)

SWEET HOT MUSTARD

SO FLAVORFUL BUT YET SO EASY

1 cup	brown sugar	250 mL
½ cup	dry mustard	125 mL
2 tbsp.	flour	30 mL
4	eggs	4
⅔ cup	vinegar	150 mL
⅔ cup	water	150 mL

- In a saucepan, combine sugar, mustard, flour and eggs. Cook over medium heat until smooth and well combined. Gradually stir in vinegar and water. Stir and cook until thickened.

SERVING SUGGESTIONS Spread on bread for any meat sandwiches, add to salad dressings or pass with ham and pork entrées.

YIELD *2 CUPS (500 ML)*

BARBECUE SAUCE

GREAT FLAVOR AND CONVENIENT TO HAVE ON HAND AS REQUIRED

1 cup	ketchup	250 mL
¼ cup	steak sauce	60 mL
¼ cup	brown sugar	60 mL
¼ cup	cider vinegar	60 mL
½ cup	water	125 mL
1 tsp.	Worcestershire sauce	5 mL
2	garlic cloves, crushed	2
1 tsp.	salt	5 mL

- Combine all ingredients in a blender.
- Place in a glass jar and refrigerate until needed.

YIELD *2 CUPS (500 ML)*

Honey Mustard Sauce

ADDS AN EXTRA SPECIAL TOUCH TO BARBECUED CHICKEN OR FRANKFURTERS

2 tbsp.	dry mustard	30 mL
¼ cup	sugar	60 mL
2 tbsp.	vinegar	30 mL
2 tbsp.	honey	30 mL
	pinch of salt	

- In a saucepan, combine the mustard, sugar and vinegar. Mix until smooth.
- Add the honey and salt.
- Place on medium heat and stir until sauce boils and thickens.

YIELD   *⅔ CUP (150 ML) SAUCE*

Seafood Sauce

YOUR JAR WILL NEVER HAVE TO BE EMPTY ANYMORE

½ cup	ketchup	125 mL
½ tsp.	Tabasco sauce	2 mL
⅓ cup	horseradish	75 mL
1 tbsp.	cider vinegar	15 mL
2 tbsp.	vegetable oil	30 mL

- In a blender, combine all the ingredients. Blend.
- Place in a container and refrigerate.
- Serve with cooked shrimp, crab or scallops.

YIELD   *1 CUP (250 ML)*

HINT   Rinse out nearly empty bottles of ketchup and steak sauce with vinegar or water to avoid waste.

Horseradish Jelly

A GREAT ACCOMPANIMENT TO ROAST BEEF!

3 cups	sugar	750 mL
1 cup	prepared horseradish	250 mL
¾ cup	water	175 mL
½ cup	vinegar	125 mL
2 oz.	pectin crystals	57 g
¼ tsp.	butter	1 mL

- Place sugar in a bowl. Set aside.
- In a large saucepan, combine horseradish, water and vinegar. Stir in pectin. Bring to a boil, stirring constantly. Add sugar. Mix well. Bring to a rolling boil and boil for 1 minute. Add butter to reduce foaming.
- Remove from heat. Skim off foam. Pour into sterilized 1-cup (250 mL) jars. Seal.

YIELD   *4 CUPS (1 L)*

APPLE CHUTNEY

AN EXCELLENT USE OF A BOUNTIFUL APPLE HARVEST!

5 cups	peeled, chopped apples	1.25 L
½ cup	raisins	125 mL
2½ cups	brown sugar	625 mL
1 cup	cider vinegar	250 mL
1	medium onion, chopped	1
¼ cup	grated ginger	60 mL
5	dried red chilies, crushed (optional)	5
½ tsp.	ground cloves	2 mL
½ tsp.	nutmeg	2 mL
½ tsp.	salt	2 mL

- In a large bowl, combine the apples and raisins.
- In a large pot, combine the brown sugar, vinegar, onion, ginger, chilies and spices. Simmer for 10 minutes. Add the apple mixture. Simmer for an additional 15 minutes, or until apples are translucent.
- Pour chutney into sterilized jars. Place in a warm oven for 10 minutes to seal, or store chutney in the refrigerator.

YIELD   *APPROXIMATELY 6 CUPS (1.5 L)*

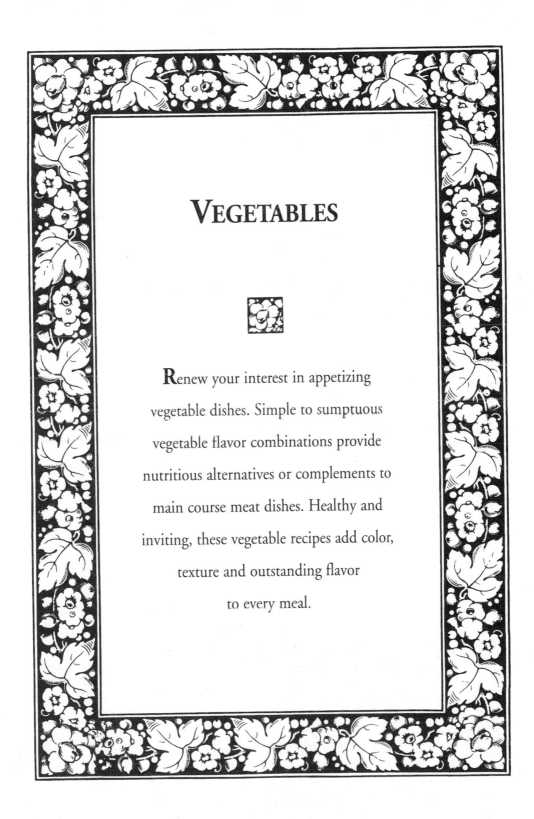

VEGETABLES

Renew your interest in appetizing
vegetable dishes. Simple to sumptuous
vegetable flavor combinations provide
nutritious alternatives or complements to
main course meat dishes. Healthy and
inviting, these vegetable recipes add color,
texture and outstanding flavor
to every meal.

LEMON GARLIC ASPARAGUS

THIS WILL GARNER RAVE REVIEWS

2	medium onions, sliced	2
3	garlic cloves, crushed	3
1 tsp.	grated lemon rind	5 mL
½ tsp.	ground thyme	2 mL
1	bay leaf	1
½ tsp.	pepper	2 mL
¼ cup	lemon juice	60 mL
2 cups	chicken broth	500 mL
1 lb.	fresh asparagus spears	500 g
2 tsp.	vegetable oil	10 mL

- In a large saucepan, combine the onions, garlic, lemon rind, thyme, bay leaf, pepper, lemon juice and chicken broth. Cover and simmer for 15 minutes. Remove the bay leaf.
- Add asparagus to saucepan. If there is not enough liquid to cover the asparagus, add additional broth. Cover and simmer slowly for 10 minutes, or until asparagus is just tender. Remove asparagus and keep it warm.
- Boil down liquid in saucepan until it is reduced to half. Add vegetable oil. Pour over asparagus. Serve immediately.

YIELD   **5 SERVINGS**

SCALLOPED MUSHROOMS

AN EXCELLENT ACCOMPANIMENT TO A STEAK BARBECUE!

1 lb.	fresh mushrooms, sliced	500 g
3 tbsp.	margarine	45 mL
⅓ cup	whipping cream	75 mL
½ tsp.	salt	2 mL
¼ tsp.	pepper	1 mL
¼ tsp.	cayenne	1 mL
1 cup	grated Monterey Jack cheese	250 mL

SCALLOPED MUSHROOMS

(CONTINUED)

- In a skillet over medium heat, sauté mushrooms in margarine for 5 minutes. Add cream. Continue to cook until most of the liquid is gone. Add salt, pepper and cayenne.
- Place mushrooms in a shallow 1-quart (1 L) dish. Sprinkle cheese over top.
- Bake at 350°F (180°C) for 12 minutes, or until cheese is melted and golden brown.

NOTE   This recipe can easily be doubled or tripled.

YIELD   **4 SERVINGS**

SPINACH BAKE

EQUALLY GOOD PREPARED AS APPETIZERS

10 oz.	pkg. frozen chopped spinach, thawed and drained	300 g
4 oz.	pkg. stuffing mix with seasonings	120 g
3	eggs, well beaten	3
1	medium onion, finely chopped	1
½ cup	butter, melted	125 mL
½ cup	grated Parmesan cheese	125 mL
½ tsp.	garlic powder	2 mL
½ tsp.	pepper	2 mL
½ tsp.	salt	2 mL
½ tsp.	dried thyme	2 mL

- In a large mixing bowl, combine all ingredients.
- Place in a 1½-quart (1.5 L) greased shallow baking dish.
- Bake at 350°F (180°C) for 30 minutes, or until thoroughly heated.

VARIATIONS   This mixture also makes excellent appetizers. After mixing all ingredients, chill. Shape into bite-sized balls. Place on a lightly greased cookie sheet. Bake at 350°F (180°C) for 20 minutes. Serve hot.

YIELD   **A 6-SERVING SIDE DISH OR 60 APPETIZERS.**

CORN/PEPPER CASSEROLE
VERY COLORFUL AND TASTY

2 tbsp.	butter	30 mL
4	green onions, chopped	4
1	green pepper, chopped	1
1	red pepper, chopped	1
19 oz.	can corn kernels, drained	540 g
1 tbsp.	cream	15 mL
½ tsp.	salt	2 mL
¼ tsp.	pepper	1 mL
½ cup	grated Cheddar cheese	125 mL
1 tbsp.	chopped parsley	15 mL

- In a skillet, melt butter. Add onions, peppers and corn kernels. Cook 2 minutes. Remove from heat.
- Add cream. Season with salt and pepper.
- Pour into a 2-quart (2 L) shallow ovenproof dish.
- Combine cheese and parsley. Sprinkle over the top.
- Cover. Bake at 350°F (180°C) for 15 minutes, or until heated through.

YIELD   **8 SERVINGS**

See photograph on page 121.

BROCCOLI ONION CASSEROLE
AN EXCELLENT SIDE DISH TO SERVE WITH ROAST BEEF OR PORK

1 lb.	broccoli	500 g
3	medium cooking onions	3
¼ cup	butter	60 mL
2 tbsp.	flour	30 mL
¼ tsp.	salt	1 mL
¼ tsp.	pepper	1 mL
1 cup	milk	250 mL
3 oz.	cream cheese	85 g
1 cup	grated sharp Cheddar cheese	250 mL

BROCCOLI ONION CASSEROLE
(CONTINUED)

- Cut broccoli into bite-sized pieces. Cook in boiling water for 3 minutes, or until just tender. Drain.
- Cut onions into chunks. Blanch in boiling water for 2-3 minutes, or until just tender. Drain.
- In a saucepan, melt butter. Add flour, salt, pepper and milk. Whisk over heat until smooth. Reduce heat and blend in the cream cheese. Beat until smooth.
- Layer drained vegetables and sauce into a 2-quart (2 L) casserole.
- Sprinkle grated cheese over top. Cover.
- Bake at 350°F (180°C) for 45 minutes, or until thoroughly heated.

YIELD   *6 SERVINGS*

GLAZED VEGETABLES

A DELICIOUS DISH WHEN FRESH GARDEN VEGETABLES ARE PLENTIFUL

4	carrots	4
1	turnip	1
4	small zucchini	4
2	medium onions	2
2 tbsp.	butter	30 mL
2 tsp.	sugar	10 mL
½ tsp.	salt	2 mL
¼ tsp.	pepper	1 mL

- Peel carrots and turnip. Cut diagonally into thin slices.
- Slice unpeeled zucchini diagonally.
- Peel onions. Cut into wedges.
- Place carrots in a large saucepan. Add water to pan to a depth of ¼" (6 mm). Add butter, sugar, salt and pepper.
- Cover pan and bring to a boil. Add turnips and return to a boil. Add onions and return to a boil. Add zucchini and return to a boil.
- Reduce heat and simmer, covered, until vegetables are just tender, about 3-5 minutes.

YIELD   *8-10 SERVINGS*

101

MIXED VEGETABLE CASSEROLE

A DELICIOUS COMBINATION FOR COMPANY

1	head cauliflower	1
1	bunch broccoli	1
8 oz.	can water chestnuts, drained	250 g
4	bacon slices	4
½ cup	chopped onion	125 mL
2 tbsp.	butter	30 mL
2 tbsp.	flour	30 mL
1½ cups	chicken broth	375 mL
1 cup	fine bread crumbs	250 mL
1 tsp.	salt	5 mL
½ tsp.	pepper	2 mL
½ tsp.	dried thyme	2 mL
½ tsp.	garlic powder	2 mL
½ tsp.	dried sweet basil	2 mL
2 tbsp.	butter, melted	30 mL

- Cut cauliflower and broccoli in florets. In a saucepan, steam just until tender, about 5 minutes. Drain. Place into a greased 1½-quart (1.5 L) casserole. Place water chestnuts on top.
- In a skillet, fry bacon until crisp. Cut into pieces and layer in casserole.
- Sauté onions until translucent. Place in casserole.
- In a saucepan, melt 2 tbsp. (30 mL) butter. Add the flour and mix well. Add the chicken broth and cook until thickened. Pour over vegetables in casserole.
- In a small bowl, combine bread crumbs and spices. Pour melted butter over and mix well. Spread crumb mixture over casserole.
- Bake at 350°F (180°C) for 45 minutes, or until thoroughly heated.

YIELD   **8-10 SERVINGS**

Turnip carrot puff

A GREAT ACCOMPANIMENT TO POULTRY DISHES

2 cups	chopped turnip	500 mL
2½ cups	chopped carrots	625 mL
¼ cup	chopped onion	60 mL
1½ cups	chicken stock	375 mL
1 tbsp.	butter	15 mL
1 tbsp.	brown sugar	15 mL
¼ tsp.	nutmeg	1 mL
2	eggs	2
2 tbsp.	flour	30 mL
1 tsp.	baking powder	5 mL
¼ tsp.	salt	1 mL
¼ tsp.	pepper	1 mL
	brown sugar and chopped nuts (optional)	

- In a large saucepan, combine the turnip, carrots, onion, chicken stock, butter and brown sugar. Bring to a boil, reduce heat and simmer until vegetables are tender.
- Drain off and save the stock. Return ¼ cup (60 mL) to vegetables and save the remainder for soup.
- Mash the vegetables.
- Add nutmeg, eggs, flour, baking powder, salt and pepper. Whip well.
- Place vegetables in a greased 1-quart (1 L) casserole. If desired, sprinkle brown sugar and nuts on the top.
- Bake at 350°F (180°C) for 45 minutes, or until thoroughly heated.

YIELD   *8 SERVINGS*

CREOLE LIMA BEANS

THIS IS NOT ONLY A SIDE DISH, IT IS GREAT SERVED WITH TOAST FOR LUNCH

4	slices bacon	4
1	medium onion, chopped	1
¼ cup	chopped green pepper	60 mL
1	garlic clove, minced	1
2 cups	canned tomatoes	500 mL
1 tsp.	sugar	5 mL
½ tsp.	ground thyme	2 mL
14 oz.	can baby lima beans, drained	398 mL
¼ tsp.	salt	1 mL
¼ tsp.	pepper	1 mL
1 tbsp.	Parmesan cheese	15 mL

- In a large skillet, sauté the bacon until crisp. Remove from pan. Crumble and set aside.
- In the same skillet, sauté onion, pepper and garlic until tender. Add tomatoes, sugar and thyme. Cook slowly for about 15 minutes, stirring occasionally.
- Add the beans, salt and pepper. Simmer until thoroughly heated. Serve hot, sprinkled with crumbled bacon and Parmesan cheese.

YIELD   5 SERVINGS

BEAN CASSEROLE

A SUBSTANTIAL ADDITION TO A BRUNCH MENU OR BUFFET

14 oz.	can pork and beans	398 mL
14 oz.	can lima beans, drained	398 mL
14 oz.	can kidney beans	398 mL
10 oz.	can mushroom pieces and stems, drained	284 mL
8	bacon slices	8
2	medium onions, chopped	2
¼ cup	vinegar	60 mL
1 cup	brown sugar	250 mL

- In a 2½-quart (2.5 L) ovenproof casserole, combine the various beans and the mushrooms.
- In a skillet, fry bacon until crisp. Remove slices and crumble. Reserve 2 tbsp. (30 mL) of drippings.
- In reserved drippings, sauté onion.
- Return bacon to skillet along with vinegar and brown sugar. Cook slowly until thickened. Pour over bean mixture. Combine well.
- Bake at 350°F (180°C) for 1 hour.

YIELD   ***10-12 SERVINGS***

PINEAPPLE BEAN POT

SUPERB IN A SLOW COOKER, TOO

2 x 14 oz.	cans pork and beans	2 x 398 mL
14 oz.	can pineapple tidbits, drained	398 mL
1	medium onion, sliced	1
1 tbsp.	soy sauce	15 mL
1	green pepper, chopped	1
10 oz.	ham OR kielbasa sausage, cubed (optional)	300 g

- Combine all ingredients in a 2½-quart (2.5 L) casserole.
- Bake at 300°F (150°C) for 50 minutes, or until thoroughly heated.

YIELD   *8-10 SERVINGS*

CHEESE POTATOES

A POPULAR VERSION OF TWICE-BAKED POTATOES

6	baking potatoes, baked	6
¼ cup	chopped onion	60 mL
3 tbsp.	margarine	45 mL
1 cup	sour cream	250 mL
1½ cups	grated Cheddar cheese	375 mL

- Slice tops off baked potatoes. Leaving the jackets intact, scoop out the potato flesh. Place potato flesh in a bowl. Mash.
- In a skillet, sauté onion in margarine. Add to the mashed potatoes along with the sour cream and half of the cheese. Mash again. Fill potato jackets with the mashed potato mixture. Sprinkle remaining cheese on the top.
- Bake at 325°F (160°C) for 40 minutes, or until potatoes are thoroughly heated.

YIELD   *6 SERVINGS*

Deluxe potatoes

A superb brunch dish

2 lbs.	frozen hash browns	1 kg
1	large onion, chopped	1
10 oz.	can cream of celery soup	284 mL
2 cups	sour cream	500 mL
¼ cup	melted butter	60 mL
8 oz.	grated Cheddar cheese	250 g
1 tsp.	salt	5 mL
½ tsp.	pepper	2 mL
1 cup	cornflake crumbs	250 mL

- In a large mixing bowl, combine all ingredients except cornflake crumbs. Spread into a greased 9 x 13" (23 x 33 cm) pan or deep casserole. Sprinkle cornflake crumbs on top.
- Bake at 350°F (180°C) for 1 hour.

YIELD   **10 SERVINGS**

IRISH POTATOES

THIS DELICIOUS POTATO DISH IS ALSO KNOWN AS RUMBLEDYTHUMPS!

4-6 cups	cooked mashed potatoes	1-1.5 L
2 cups	shredded cabbage	500 mL
1 cup	chopped onion	250 mL
½ cup	water	125 mL
2 tbsp.	butter	30 mL
½ cup	milk	125 mL
	salt and pepper to taste	
½ cup	shredded Cheddar cheese	125 mL

- Prepare the potatoes.
- In a skillet, cook cabbage and onions in water until most of the water has evaporated. Add butter and cook until tender, about 5 minutes. Add to mashed potatoes along with milk and salt and pepper to taste. Mix well.
- Place potato mixture in a greased 2½-quart (2.5 L) casserole. Sprinkle with cheese.
- Bake at 350°F (180°C) for 40 minutes, or until heated through.

YIELD   *8 SERVINGS*

LAZY CABBAGE ROLLS

ENJOY THE TASTE OF CABBAGE ROLLS WITHOUT THE FUSS

4	bacon slices, chopped	4
1	small onion, chopped	1
19 oz.	can sauerkraut	540 mL
1 tbsp.	brown sugar	15 mL
1½ cups	raw long-grain rice	375 mL
½ tsp.	pepper	2 mL
10 oz.	can tomato soup	284 mL
2 cups	water	500 mL

- In a skillet, sauté bacon until crisp. Add onions. Cook until onions are translucent. Drain off fat.
- Rinse sauerkraut. Drain well.
- In a mixing bowl, combine onions, bacon, sauerkraut, sugar, rice and pepper.
- Combine the tomato soup and water. Add to rice mixture. Transfer to a greased 2½-quart (2.5 L) casserole. Cover.
- Bake at 350°F (180°C) for 1½ hours, or until rice is tender.

VARIATIONS   For German-style cabbage rolls, add a layer of cooked ground beef.

YIELD   **6-8 SERVINGS**

MEXICAN RICE CASSEROLE

THIS PROVES THAT RICE IS ANYTHING BUT BLAND

1 cup	long-grain rice	250 mL
2 cups	water	500 mL
½ tsp.	salt	2 mL
1 tsp.	vinegar	5 mL
10 oz.	can condensed cream of celery soup	284 mL
1 cup	sour cream	250 mL
4 oz.	can diced green chilies	113 mL
10 oz.	can mushroom pieces and stems, drained	284 mL
1½ cups	grated sharp Cheddar cheese	375 mL
1 tsp.	Tabasco sauce	5 mL

- In a large saucepan, combine rice, water, salt and vinegar. Bring to a boil; cover, and boil gently until rice is tender, about 20 minutes.
- Add remaining ingredients. Mix well.
- Place rice mixture in a greased 2-quart (2 L) casserole.
- Bake, covered, at 350°F (180°C) for 30 minutes, or until thoroughly heated.

YIELD   *8 SERVINGS*

MAIN COURSES

Enjoy your favorite flavors from
grandma's kitchen. The tantalizing dishes
made by grandmas from many cultures
are adapted to the busy lifestyles of
grandmas today. Some shortcuts and
convenience foods enable you to quickly
and easily make mouth-watering
family favorites.

NEW ENGLAND BOILED DINNER

A SUNDAY DINNER SPECIALTY THAT REQUIRES LITTLE WATCHING

3 lbs.	boneless round rump beef roast	1.5 kg
1 tbsp.	vegetable oil	15 mL
2 cups	beef bouillon	500 mL
2 tbsp.	horseradish	30 mL
1	bay leaf	1
2	garlic cloves, minced	2
6	medium carrots, cut into 1" (2.5 cm) pieces	6
1	medium turnip, peeled and cut into wedges	1
6	medium potatoes, peeled and quartered	6
1	small cabbage, cut into wedges	1
	water	

- In a large, heavy saucepan, brown meat in oil.
- Add bouillon, horseradish, bay leaf and garlic. Cover and cook over low heat for 2 hours. Remove bay leaf.
- Add carrots, turnips and potatoes. Cook for 30 minutes. Add cabbage wedges. Cook 30 more minutes, or until vegetables are tender.
- As vegetables cook, add water in small amounts, if required, to maintain adequate moisture in saucepan.
- To serve, place beef on a large platter. Surround with vegetables.

YIELD   *8 SERVINGS*

SHISH KEBABS

GREAT FOR AN INFORMAL OUTDOOR DINNER — LET GUESTS PREPARE AND
COOK THEIR OWN

2 lbs.	beef sirloin	1 kg
½ cup	vegetable oil	125 mL
½ cup	lemon juice	125 mL
½ cup	finely chopped onion	125 mL
1 tsp.	salt	5 mL
½ tsp.	pepper	2 mL
1 tsp.	Worcestershire sauce	5 mL
1	bay leaf	1
	assorted vegetables (cherry tomatoes, peppers, mushrooms, small onions)	

- A day in advance of serving, cut beef into uniform cubes. Combine remaining ingredients, except vegetables, to make a marinade. Marinate beef overnight.
- Remove beef cubes from marinade.
- Prepare vegetables by washing and, if necessary, cutting into pieces.
- On skewers, alternate pieces of meat with vegetables.
- Broil skewered meat and vegetables over coals or under the broiler for about 5 minutes, or until done as desired.

VARIATION   For people who prefer their beef well done, cook beef and vegetables on separate skewers so vegetables don't over cook. Serve each person 1 or more vegetable skewers and meat skewers.

YIELD   **6 SERVINGS**

REUBEN CASSEROLE

A REAL TREAT FOR REUBEN SANDWICH FANS!

8 oz.	wide egg noodles	250 g
1 tbsp.	butter	15 mL
4	bacon slices, diced	4
1	onion, chopped	1
14 oz.	can sauerkraut, drained and rinsed	398 mL
½ cup	water	125 mL
	salt and pepper to taste	
8 oz.	cubed OR chopped corned beef	250 g
2	medium tomatoes, chopped	2
½ cup	Thousand Island dressing	125 mL
8 oz.	Swiss cheese, grated	250 g
½ tsp.	caraway seeds (optional)	2 mL

• Cook noodles according to package directions. Drain. Add butter. Mix. Spread into a greased 9 x 13" (23 x 33 cm) baking dish.
• In a skillet, sauté the bacon. Add the onions. Cook until onions are translucent. Pour off all but 1 tbsp. (15 mL) of drippings. Add the sauerkraut and water. Simmer for 30 minutes. Add salt and pepper to taste.
• Layer the sauerkraut mixture over the noodles. Continue to layer with the corned beef, tomatoes, dressing and cheese.
• If desired, sprinkle with caraway seeds.
• Bake, covered, at 350°F (180°C) for 40 minutes. Uncover and continue to bake for an additional 15 minutes.

YIELD   *8 SERVINGS*

INDIVIDUAL MEAT LOAVES

FLAVORFUL LITTLE LOAVES THAT CAN BE MADE AHEAD AND FROZEN,
GREAT TASTE AND GREAT CONVENIENCE

1 lb.	lean ground beef	500 g
1	egg, slightly beaten	1
1 cup	fresh bread crumbs	250 mL
½ cup	finely chopped onion	125 mL
2 tbsp.	creamed horseradish	30 mL
1 tsp.	salt	5 mL
1 tsp.	dry mustard	5 mL
1½ tbsp.	milk	22 mL
¼ cup	ketchup	60 mL

- In a mixing bowl, combine beef, eggs, crumbs and onion.
- Add remaining ingredients. Combine well.
- Shape meat mixture into 6 individual oval loaves.
- Place loaves in greased shallow pan or in mini loaf pans.
- If desired, spread the tops of each loaf with more ketchup.
- Bake at 375°F (190°C) for 35 minutes, or until done.

YIELD   *6, 2 X 4" (6 X 10 CM) MEAT LOAVES*

See photograph on page 121.

PORCUPINE MEAT BALLS

ANOTHER OF GRANDMA'S FAVORITES ENJOYED BY ALL

1 lb.	lean ground beef	500 g
1	small onion, finely chopped	1
⅓ cup	rice	75 mL
½ tsp.	salt	2 mL
½ tsp.	pepper	2 mL
1	egg	1
½ cup	flour	125 mL
2 tbsp.	vegetable oil	30 mL
10 oz.	can tomato soup	284 mL
1 cup	water	250 mL

- In a mixing bowl, combine beef, onion, rice, salt, pepper and egg.
- Shape into 1" (2.5 cm) balls. Roll each ball in flour and brown in hot oil in a skillet.
- Place meatballs in a 2-quart (2 L) casserole.
- Combine the soup and water. Pour over the meatballs.
- Bake at 350°F (180°C) for 1 hour, or until rice is tender. Add more water during baking if necessary.

YIELD   4-6 SERVINGS

BEEF BURGER JELLY ROLL

THE PRESENTATION MAKES THIS A GOOD DISH TO INCLUDE IN A BUFFET

1 lb.	lean ground beef	500 g
¼ cup	chopped onion	60 mL
½ cup	fine bread crumbs	125 mL
½ tsp.	salt	2 mL
½ tsp.	pepper	2 mL
½ tsp.	garlic powder	2 mL
1	egg	1
1 tbsp.	water	15 mL
10 oz.	pkg. frozen spinach	284 g
1 cup	chopped mushrooms	250 mL
½ cup	chopped onion	125 mL
1 tbsp.	chopped fresh parsley	15 mL
½ cup	shredded mozzarella cheese	125 mL
¼ cup	bread crumbs	60 mL
½ tsp.	salt	2 mL
½ tsp.	pepper	2 mL

- In a mixing bowl, combine the beef, onion and bread crumbs. Mix well. Add the salt, pepper, garlic powder, egg and water. Combine well.
- Spread beef evenly on a 12 x 18" (30 x 45 cm) sheet of waxed paper.
- Cook spinach according to package directions. Squeeze out moisture.
- In a skillet sauté the mushrooms and onions until onions are translucent. Remove from heat.
- To the mushroom mixture, add the cooked spinach, parsley, cheese, bread crumbs, salt and pepper. Mix well.
- Spread the mushroom mixture evenly over the beef.
- Taking the waxed paper from one of the short ends, roll the beef and filling like a jelly roll. Carefully transfer to a greased 9 x 13" (23 x 33 cm) pan, being sure to remove the waxed paper.
- Bake at 325°F (160°C), uncovered, for 1 hour. Let sit for 5 minutes before cutting.

SERVING SUGGESTION Transfer beef roll to a serving dish; decorate with chili sauce on top and cherry tomatoes and parsley on the sides.

YIELD ***6 SERVINGS***

GROUND BEEF STROGANOFF

A MODERN VERSION OF A CLASSIC DISH

1 tbsp.	vegetable oil	15 mL
1 lb.	lean ground beef	500 g
1	large onion, chopped	1
2	garlic cloves, minced	2
10 oz.	can mushroom pieces, drained	284 mL
2 cups	beef broth	500 mL
1 cup	sour cream	250 mL
2 tbsp.	flour	30 mL

- In a large skillet, heat oil and brown ground beef. Add onion, garlic and mushrooms. Continue to sauté until onions are translucent.
- Add beef broth. Mix well.
- Combine sour cream and flour. Add to skillet.
- Simmer for approximately 30 minutes, stirring occasionally.

***SERVING
SUGGESTION*** Serve over egg noodles with a side salad.

YIELD **5-6 SERVINGS**

BEEF MUSHROOM CUPS

TREAT YOUR FAMILY OR FRIENDS TO AN INTERESTING LUNCHEON OR SNACK

12	slices of bread, crust removed	12
12 oz.	lean ground beef	375 g
1	small onion, chopped	1
½	green pepper, chopped	½
1	garlic clove, minced	1
10 oz.	can cream of mushroom soup	284 mL
1 cup	grated Cheddar cheese	250 mL

BEEF MUSHROOM CUPS
(CONTINUED)

- Press bread slices into muffin cups in a muffin tin.
- In a skillet, brown the beef. Add the onion, pepper and garlic. Cook until onion is translucent. Add mushroom soup. Simmer for 15 minutes, stirring occasionally. Remove from heat.
- Divide beef mixture evenly into bread cups in muffin tin. Sprinkle each cup with cheese.
- Bake at 350°F (180°C) for 15-20 minutes, or until bread is lightly toasted and cheese is melted.

YIELD   *6 SERVINGS*

BEEF NACHO CASSEROLE
THANK THE MEXICANS FOR THEIR INFLUENCE IN OUR COOKING

1 tbsp.	vegetable oil	15 mL
1 lb.	lean ground beef	500 g
1½ cups	chunky salsa	375 mL
12 oz.	can kernel corn	341 mL
¾ cup	mayonnaise-type salad dressing	175 mL
1 tbsp.	chili powder	15 mL
2 cups	crushed nachos chips	500 mL
2 cups	shredded Colby OR Monterey Jack cheese	500 mL

- In a skillet, heat vegetable oil and sauté beef until no longer pink. Remove from heat.
- Add salsa, corn, salad dressing and chili powder to beef. Mix well.
- Place beef mixture into a greased 2½-quart (2.5 L) casserole.
- Top beef mixture with crushed nachos and then cheese.
- Cover. Bake at 350°F (180°C) for 45 minutes, until thoroughly heated.

NOTE   Mild, medium, or hot salsa may be used depending on preference.

YIELD   *8 SERVINGS*

BEEF CHOW MEIN CASSEROLE

A FAMILY FAVORITE FOR BUSY DAYS

1 tbsp.	vegetable oil	15 mL
1 lb.	lean ground beef	500 g
3	celery stalks, chopped	3
1	large onion, chopped	1
¼ tsp.	salt	1 mL
¼ tsp.	pepper	1 mL
10 oz.	can cream of chicken soup	284 mL
10 oz.	can cream of mushroom soup	284 mL
2 tbsp.	soy sauce	30 mL
½ cup	instant cooking rice	125 mL
1 cup	chow mein noodles	250 mL

- In a skillet, heat oil and sauté ground beef. Add celery and onion and continue to cook until vegetables are translucent. Remove from heat.
- Add remaining ingredients, except noodles. Mix well.
- Pour into a 2½-quart (2.5 L) casserole.
- Bake, uncovered, at 350°F (180°C) for ½ hour.
- Remove from oven and sprinkle noodles over casserole. Cover.
- Reduce heat to 300°F (150°C) and continue to bake for another ½ hour.

YIELD   4-6 SERVINGS

MAIN COURSE

Individual Meat Loaves, page 115
Corn/Pepper Casserole, page 100
Tomato Basil Bread, page 16

ZUCCHINI LASAGNE

INDIFFERENT TO ZUCCHINI? YOU'LL LOVE THIS DISH

2 tbsp.	vegetable oil	30 mL
1 lb.	lean ground beef	500 g
1	medium onion, chopped	1
2	garlic cloves, minced	2
14 oz.	can spaghetti sauce	398 mL
5½ oz.	can tomato paste	156 mL
2	eggs	2
8 oz.	2% cottage cheese	250 g
3	medium zucchini, sliced	3
2 tbsp.	flour	30 mL
8 oz.	mozzarella cheese, grated	250 g
⅓ cup	bread crumbs	75 mL

- In a large skillet, heat oil and sauté the beef until no longer pink. Add the onions and garlic and continue to cook until onions are translucent. Drain off excess drippings.
- Add spaghetti sauce and tomato paste. Bring to a boil; reduce heat and simmer for 20 minutes.
- In a small bowl, combine eggs and cottage cheese.
- In an 8 x 12" (20 x 30 cm) lightly greased baking dish, layer half of the zucchini slices. Sprinkle with 1 tbsp. (15 mL) of flour. Layer with egg cheese mixture.
- Over cheese mixture, layer remaining half of zucchini slices. Sprinkle with the other tbsp. (15 mL) of flour. Layer with meat mixture. Cover.
- Bake at 325°F (160°C) for 1 hour, or until zucchini is tender.
- Meanwhile, combine mozzarella cheese and bread crumbs.
- Remove lasagne from oven, sprinkle with mozzarella mixture. Return lasagne, uncovered, to oven for an additional 15 minutes, or until cheese is melted.
- Let stand for 10 minutes before cutting to serve.

YIELD   *8 SERVINGS*

STUFFED PORK ROAST

ELEGANT AND TASTY — YOU'LL BE PROUD TO SERVE IT!

2 lb.	boneless pork loin roast	1 kg
½ cup	dried apricots	125 mL
½ cup	pitted prunes	125 mL
3	red cooking apples	3
¼ cup	lemon juice	60 mL
¼ cup	apricot jam	60 mL
2 tbsp.	Dijon mustard	30 mL
1 tsp.	salt	5 mL
1 tbsp.	orange juice	15 mL
3 tbsp.	butter	45 mL
2 tbsp.	brown sugar	30 mL
¼ tsp.	cinnamon	1 mL
1 cup	water	250 mL

- Cut loin roast horizontally in half lengthwise, but not quite all the way through. Arrange a layer of overlapping apricots and a layer of overlapping prunes down the center of half of the roast. Fold the other half over the fruit and secure in place with kitchen string.
- Place roast on a rack in a large open roasting pan.
- Bake at 325°F (160°C) for 1 hour.
- Meanwhile, core apples and cut into wedges. Sprinkle with lemon juice.
- After roast has cooked for 1 hour, add apple wedges to roasting pan.
- Combine apricot jam, mustard, salt and juice. Brush over roast.
- Melt butter. Combine with brown sugar and cinnamon. Brush over apples.
- Bake roast for another hour. While baking, continue to brush pork with mustard sauce and apples with brown sugar sauce at 15 minute intervals.
- Remove roast from oven. Cut off kitchen string. Surround roast with apples. Keep warm.
- To drippings in roasting pan, add 1 cup (250 mL) of water, stirring to loosen drippings. Cook over medium heat until mixture boils. Remove from heat.
- Serve roast and fruit with pan drippings on the side.

YIELD   *8 SERVINGS*

JAMAICAN PORK

A PLEASANT SWEET AND SOUR FLAVOR FOR PORK

1 lb.	pork tenderloin	500 g
1 tbsp.	vegetable oil	15 mL
1	medium onion, chopped	1
1	garlic clove, minced	1
2 tbsp.	brown sugar	30 mL
2 tbsp.	cornstarch	30 mL
⅓ cup	water	75 mL
2 tbsp.	vinegar	30 mL
2 tbsp.	soy sauce	30 mL
⅓ cup	ketchup	75 mL
14 oz.	can pineapple tidbits, drained, reserve syrup	398 mL
1	green pepper, chopped (optional)	1

- Cut tenderloin into bite-sized pieces. In a skillet, heat oil and brown the pork. Add the onion and garlic. Sauté until translucent. Place in a 1½-quart (1.5 L) lightly greased casserole.
- In a small saucepan, combine the brown sugar and cornstarch. Add the water, vinegar, soy sauce, ketchup and reserved pineapple syrup. Cook over low heat, stirring until smooth and thick. Simmer for 2 minutes. Pour over pork.
- Bake at 350°F (180°C) for 30 minutes. Add pineapple tidbits and green pepper. Bake for an additional 30 minutes. Serve hot over a bed of rice.

YIELD   *4 SERVINGS*

SWEET AND SPICY PORK

A LITTLE BIT DIFFERENT, BUT VERY SPECIAL!

1½ lbs.	pork tenderloin	700 g
¾ cup	brown sugar	175 mL
¾ cup	lemon juice	175 mL
1½ tsp.	pepper	7 mL
½ tsp.	ground cumin	2 mL
½ tsp.	ground allspice	2 mL
½ tsp.	ground cloves	2 mL

- Slice tenderloin into slices about ¾" (2 cm) thick.
- In a glass bowl, combine the remaining ingredients to make a marinade.
- Place sliced pork in marinade. Marinate for 2-3 hours.
- Place pork on a broiler rack or on a barbecue. Broil about 6" (15 cm) from heat, about 5 minutes on each side, or until tender. While broiling, brush with marinade.
- Serve over a bed of rice or egg noodles.

YIELD   *6 SERVINGS*

STUFFED SPARERIBS

ESPECIALLY HEARTY SERVED WITH BOILED NEW POTATOES

3 tbsp.	margarine	45 mL
1	medium onion, chopped	1
3	celery stalks, chopped	3
1	apple, chopped	1
2 tbsp.	chopped fresh parsley	30 mL
1 tsp.	salt	5 mL
½ tsp.	pepper	2 mL
1 tsp.	thyme	5 mL
3 cups	bread crumbs	750 mL
	water	
4 lbs.	spareribs, cut into 2 equal pieces	1.8 kg

- In a skillet, heat margarine and sauté the onion and celery until translucent. Add apple and spices to onion mixture.
- In a mixing bowl, combine onion mixture and bread crumbs. Add only enough water to hold dressing together.
- Place half the ribs with meaty side down. Cover with dressing. Place remaining ribs on top with meaty side up. Tie ribs and dressing together with kitchen string. Place in a roasting pan.
- Bake at 350°F (180°C) for 1½-2 hours, or until ribs are tender. Turn ribs over halfway through the baking time. While baking, baste with drippings.

YIELD   *6 SERVINGS*

CHICKEN CASHEW STIR-FRY

LOOKING FOR A QUICK, DELICIOUS DINNER BEFORE RUSHING OFF FOR THE EVENING? THIS IS IT

SOY SHERRY MARINADE:

2 tbsp.	soy sauce	30 mL
2 tbsp.	sherry	30 mL
2 tsp.	cornstarch	10 mL

2	chicken breasts (4 halves), skinned, boned, and cut into bite-sized pieces	2
1 tbsp.	vegetable oil	15 mL
2	celery stalks, chopped	2
8	button mushrooms, sliced	8
4	green onions, chopped	4
6 oz.	pkg. frozen pea pods	170 g
1	green pepper, chopped	1
2	garlic cloves, crushed	2
1 cup	chicken broth	250 mL
½ cup	cashews	125 mL

- About an hour before serving, combine marinade ingredients in a glass bowl. Add chicken pieces. Let sit for at least an hour.
- In a wok or large skillet, heat oil and stir-fry celery, mushrooms, onions, pea pods and pepper for 2 minutes. Set crisp vegetables aside.
- Add garlic and drained chicken pieces to wok. Stir-fry chicken in small batches, until it becomes firm and white, about 2-3 minutes per batch. Set chicken aside and keep warm.
- Add marinade and chicken broth to wok. Stir and cook until liquid thickens.
- Add chicken and reserved vegetables. Sprinkle with cashews. Mix well. Serve over a bed of rice.

YIELD   *4 SERVINGS*

Poulet de la France

Guaranteed to impress your guests!

½ cup	flour	125 mL
½ tsp.	salt	2 mL
1 tbsp.	paprika	15 mL
½ tsp.	pepper	2 mL
½ tsp.	garlic powder	2 mL
2	chicken breasts (4 halves), boned, cut into pieces	2
2 tbsp.	oil	30 mL
1 cup	sliced fresh mushrooms	250 mL
10 oz.	can cream of mushroom soup	284 mL
½ cup	chicken broth	125 mL
½ cup	dry white wine	125 mL
½ cup	orange juice	125 mL
1 tbsp.	grated fresh ginger	15 mL
1 tbsp.	brown sugar	15 mL
1 tbsp.	orange rind	15 mL
2 cups	sliced carrots	500 mL
1 cup	chopped celery	250 mL

- Combine the flour, salt, paprika, pepper and garlic powder in a plastic bag. Add chicken pieces. Shake to coat.
- In a Dutch oven, heat oil and brown chicken pieces. Add sliced mushrooms and sauté until soft. Turn heat down.
- Add mushroom soup, chicken broth, wine, orange juice, ginger and brown sugar. Simmer, covered, for 30 minutes.
- Meanwhile, steam the carrots and celery with the orange rind for about 8 minutes. Add to the chicken. Simmer for another 40 minutes, or until vegetables and chicken are tender. Serve hot on a bed of rice.

YIELD   *6 SERVINGS*

ONE-DISH CHICKEN AND RICE

MAKE IN THE MORNING — COOK IN THE LATE AFTERNOON!

1 cup	long-grain rice	250 mL
½ cup	chopped onion	125 mL
½ cup	chopped celery	125 mL
1 cup	sliced carrots	250 mL
3	chicken breasts (6 halves), boned	3
10 oz.	can of chicken soup	284 mL
½ cup	water	125 mL
½ cup	white wine	125 mL

- In a greased 2-quart (2 L) casserole, layer the rice, the vegetables and chicken.
- Combine the soup, water and wine. Pour over layers in casserole.
- Refrigerate until an hour and a half before serving.
- Bake at 350°F (180°C) for an hour and a half.

YIELD   6 SERVINGS

CHICKEN RICE CASSEROLE

A DELIGHTFUL BLEND OF FLAVORS

1 cup	long-grain rice	250 mL
3 cups	diced, cooked chicken	750 mL
14 oz.	can cut green beans, drained	398 mL
10 oz.	can cream of celery soup	284 mL
1 cup	mayonnaise	250 mL
1	medium onion, chopped	1
1	red pepper, chopped	1
8 oz.	can water chestnuts, drained and sliced	250 mL

- Cook rice according to package directions.
- In a large mixing bowl, combine rice with remaining ingredients. Place in a lightly greased 2-quart (2 L) casserole. Cover.
- Bake at 350°F (180°C) for 45 minutes.

YIELD   6-8 SERVINGS

CHICKEN PASTA SUPRÊME

A DELIGHTFUL BLEND OF FLAVORS AND TEXTURES THAT IS SURE TO PLEASE!

3	chicken breasts (6 halves)	3
1 cup	small pasta (shells, spirals, noodles, etc.)	250 mL
1 tbsp.	vegetable oil	15 mL
1	small onion, chopped	1
2	celery stalks, chopped	2
1 cup	sliced mushrooms (optional)	250 mL
1 cup	cubed mozzarella cheese	250 mL
10 oz.	can cream of chicken soup	284 mL
1 cup	milk	250 mL
¾ cup	mayonnaise	175 mL
1 tbsp.	lemon juice	15 mL
½ cup	crushed cornflakes	125 mL
½ cup	slivered almonds	125 mL

- In a saucepan, bring enough water to cover chicken breasts to a simmer; add chicken and simmer until just cooked, until meat is firm to the touch and white throughout. Cool. Bone and cut in 1" (2.5 cm) pieces.
- Cook the pasta in salted water according to package directions. Drain and cool.
- In a skillet, heat oil and sauté the onion, celery and mushrooms until onions are translucent.
- In a large bowl, combine the chicken pieces, pasta and vegetables. Add the cheese.
- In a small bowl, combine the chicken soup and milk. Add the mayonnaise and lemon juice. Mix well. Add to the chicken mixture.
- Pour the chicken mixture into a greased 2-quart (2 L) casserole.
- Top with cornflakes and almonds.
- Bake at 350°F (180°C) for 1 hour, or until thoroughly heated.

VARIATIONS   Poach chicken breasts in water, seasoned with salt, pepper and appropriate herbs (thyme, oregano, tarragon, savory, etc.), or in chicken broth or white wine.

NOTE   This casserole freezes well.

YIELD   *6-8 SERVINGS*

CHICKEN 'N' TRIMMINGS

THIS COULD EASILY BECOME A REQUEST FOR THANKSGIVING!

3	chicken breasts (6 halves), skinned, boned	3
4 oz.	Swiss cheese, grated	115 g
2 cups	dry bread crumbs	500 mL
½ tsp.	salt	2 mL
½ tsp.	pepper	2 mL
1 tsp.	dried sage	5 mL
½ tsp.	poultry seasoning	2 mL
10 oz.	can condensed cream of chicken soup	284 mL
14 oz.	can cranberry sauce	398 mL

- Grease a 9 x 13" (23 x 33 cm) pan.
- Cut chicken breasts into quarters. Layer in the bottom of the pan.
- Sprinkle grated cheese evenly over chicken.
- Layer bread crumbs over cheese.
- Sprinkle with seasonings.
- Continue to layer with chicken soup and then cranberry sauce.
- Cover with foil.
- Bake at 350°F (180°C) for 1 hour.

YIELD   **6 SERVINGS**

THAI THIGHS

A TASTE OF ASIAN COOKING WITH LITTLE FUSS BUT GREAT RESULTS!

2 lbs.	chicken thighs, skinned	1 kg

PEANUT GINGER SAUCE:

½	medium onion, chopped	½
2	garlic cloves, minced	2
¼ cup	hoisin sauce	60 mL
1 tbsp.	peanut butter	15 mL
1 tsp.	ground ginger	5 mL
1 tbsp.	soy sauce	15 mL
1 tbsp.	sesame oil	15 mL
1 tbsp.	lemon juice	15 mL
½ tsp.	Tabasco	2 mL
1 tbsp.	dried parsley flakes	15 mL

- Arrange chicken thighs in a single layer in a lightly greased baking dish.
- In a glass bowl, combine sauce ingredients. Pour over chicken. Cover.
- Bake at 350°F (180°C) for 45 minutes, basting with sauce occasionally. Remove cover and bake for an additional 15 minutes, or until chicken is tender.

YIELD   6 SERVINGS

CHICKEN DRUMSTICKS *VG.*

A GREAT IDEA FOR A PICNIC OR POTLUCK FOR COOKS WITH A BUSY SCHEDULE!

10-12	chicken drumsticks *— used chic Breasts, cut in half less cook time*	10-12

SOY PINEAPPLE MARINADE:

½ cup	water	125 mL
½ cup	soy sauce	125 mL
½ cup	sugar	125 mL
¼ cup	unsweetened pineapple juice	60 mL
2 tbsp.	vegetable oil	30 mL
1 tsp.	garlic powder	5 mL
1 tsp.	ground ginger	5 mL

- Early in the day, place drumsticks in a heavy plastic bag. Mix together all the other ingredients and pour over the drumsticks. Refrigerate. Occasionally remove bag and shake to distribute contents.
- To bake, place drumsticks in a shallow baking pan. Bake, uncovered, at 350°F (180°C) for 1-1½ hours. While baking, brush the drumsticks frequently with marinade. *With breasts — start checking after 45 mins*
- Serve hot over a bed of rice or serve cool. *thickened with flour*

NOTE   These are great make-aheads for a picnic. The recipe can be easily doubled or tripled for large crowds.

YIELD   **6 SERVINGS**

PHEASANT AND RICE

A PLEASANT CHANGE IF PHEASANT IS AVAILABLE

1 cup	rice (white, brown OR wild)	250 mL
1	pheasant, cut into pieces	1
1 tbsp.	vegetable oil	15 mL
2 tbsp.	margarine	30 mL
1	medium onion, chopped	1
2	celery stalks, chopped	2
2	chicken bouillon cubes	2
½ cup	hot water	125 mL
10 oz.	can mushroom pieces and stems, drained	284 mL
½ tsp.	salt	2 mL
¼ tsp.	pepper	1 mL

- In a large saucepan, cook rice according to package directions.
- While rice is cooking, heat oil in a skillet and brown pheasant pieces. Set aside.
- In another skillet, heat margarine and cook onion and celery until tender.
- Dissolve bouillon cubes in hot water.
- Add cooked vegetables, hot water, mushrooms, salt and pepper to rice. Mix well. Spoon into a greased deep 2½-quart (2.5 L) casserole.
- Place pheasant pieces on top of rice. Cover and bake at 350°F (180°C) for 30 minutes. Uncover and continue to bake for an additional 15 minutes, or until bird is tender, adding a small amount of water if necessary.

VARIATIONS   If pheasant is not available or is too costly, chicken is a very good substitute. For interest, vary the type of rice used or use a combination of several types of rice.

YIELD   *4-5 SERVINGS*

STUFFED FILLETS OF SOLE

THE DELICATE FLAVOR OF SOLE AT ITS BEST

2 tbsp.	butter	30 mL
1	onion, chopped	1
4 oz.	can shrimp	113 g
10 oz.	can mushrooms, drained	284 mL
8	fillets of sole	8
	salt, pepper and paprika to taste	
10 oz.	can mushroom soup	284 mL
¾ cup	dry white wine	175 mL
¾ cup	shredded Cheddar cheese	175 mL

- In a skillet, heat butter and sauté the onion, shrimp and mushrooms for 2-3 minutes.
- Sprinkle each fillet with salt, pepper and paprika.
- Divide shrimp mixture evenly among fillets and spread smoothly. Roll up fillets. Secure with a toothpick.
- Place rolls upright on a lightly greased, shallow baking pan.
- In a small mixing bowl, combine mushroom soup and wine. Pour over sole bundles. Sprinkle with cheese.
- Bake at 400°F (230°C) for 20 minutes.

NOTE   Each bundle may be baked and served in individual ovenproof baking dishes if desired.

VARIATION   Crab meat may be substituted for the shrimp.

YIELD   *6-8 SERVINGS*

GRILLED FISH STEAKS

A BARBECUE ALTERNATIVE TO POULTRY AND STEAK

HERBED LEMON MARINADE:

¼ cup	vegetable oil	60 mL
1 tbsp.	lemon juice	15 mL
1 tbsp.	finely chopped onion	15 mL
½ tsp.	salt	2 mL
½ tsp.	pepper	2 mL
½ tsp.	dried thyme, rosemary OR basil	2 mL
4	salmon steaks	4

- Early in the day, combine marinade ingredients. In a glass pan, pour marinade over fish steaks. Marinate for at least 2 hours, turning occasionally.
- Barbecue or broil to cook. To barbecue, place salmon steaks in a greased basket grill and broil about 4" (10 cm) above hot coals. Cook about 8 minutes per side, or until flesh is opaque and milky through to the center.
- To broil, place fish on a greased broiler pan. Broil 4" (10 cm) from heat for about 8 minutes per side.
- Brush steaks with marinade when they are turned over on the grill or broiler.

VARIATIONS   Halibut, sole, red snapper or trout steaks or fillets can also be done using this method. Vary the cooking time according to the thickness of the fish.

YIELD   *4 SERVINGS*

SALMON DILL LOAF

THE DILL MAKES THIS AN EXTRAORDINARY SALMON DISH

2 tbsp.	margarine	30 mL
1	medium onion, chopped	1
1 cup	chopped mushrooms	250 mL
2	celery stalks, chopped	2
1	egg, beaten	1
2 x 7½ oz.	cans salmon	2 x 225 g
1 cup	bread crumbs	250 g
⅔ cup	milk, scalded	150 mL
¼ cup	chopped fresh dillweed	60 mL
1 tsp.	pepper	5 mL

- In a skillet, heat margarine and sauté the onion, mushrooms and celery.
- In a mixing bowl, combine the egg with the sautéed vegetables. Flake the salmon and add to the vegetables, along with the salmon liquid.
- In a small bowl, combine the bread crumbs and milk. Add to the salmon mixture. Add dill and pepper. Mix well.
- Place the salmon mixture in a greased 5 x 9" (13 x 23 cm) loaf pan.
- Bake, uncovered, at 350°F (180°C) for 1 hour. Let sit 5 minutes before serving.

NOTE   If fresh dill is not available, substitute 1 tbsp. (15 mL) of dried crushed dill.

YIELD   *6 SERVINGS*

MAIN COURSE

Shrimp Jambalaya, page 141
Cheese Corn Sticks, page 13

SHRIMP JAMBALAYA

THIS IS ONE OF CREOLE COOKERY'S FINEST!

4 oz.	bacon, chopped	115 g
2	garlic cloves, minced	2
1	onion, chopped	1
1	celery stalk, chopped	1
1	green pepper, finely chopped	1
1-2	jalapeño peppers, seeded and finely chopped	1-2
2	bay leaves	2
½ tsp.	dried thyme	2 mL
2 tsp.	parsley flakes	10 mL
14 oz.	can tomatoes	398 mL
5½ oz.	can tomato paste	156 g
½ tsp.	salt	2 mL
¼ tsp.	pepper	1 mL
2 lbs.	cleaned, raw shrimp	1 kg
2 cups	cooked rice	500 mL

- In a large skillet, fry the bacon. Drain off all but 1 tbsp. (15 mL) of drippings. Add garlic, onion, celery and peppers. Cook until onion is tender.
- Add bay leaves, thyme, parsley, tomatoes, tomato paste, salt and pepper. Bring to a boil. Reduce heat and cook slowly for 20-30 minutes.
- Add shrimp and cook for 5 more minutes.
- Add rice. When thoroughly heated, serve.

VARIATION   If desired, scallops may be added, along with the shrimp.

YIELD   *6-8 SERVINGS*

See photograph on page 139.

LINGUINE WITH SEAFOOD SAUCE

SERVE WITH PRIDE AND A GREEN SALAD

2 tbsp.	margarine	30 mL
4	green onions, chopped	4
3	garlic cloves, minced	3
4 oz.	medium shrimp	115 g
4 oz.	scallops	115 g
2 tbsp.	lemon juice	30 mL
1 cup	chicken broth	250 mL
½ cup	dry white wine	125 mL
½ tsp.	dried ground tarragon	2 mL
2 tbsp.	cornstarch	30 mL
2 tbsp.	water	30 mL
12 oz.	linguine pasta	340 g
¼ cup	light sour cream	60 mL
2 tbsp.	margarine	30 mL
	lemon wedges and fresh parsley for garnish	

- In a skillet, melt margarine. Add onions and garlic and sauté. Stir in the shrimp, scallops, lemon juice, chicken broth, wine and tarragon. Heat to boiling. Reduce heat and simmer for 5 minutes.
- Combine the cornstarch with the water. Add to the seafood mixture. Stir until sauce thickens. Keep warm.
- Meanwhile, cook the linguine according to package directions. Drain. Rinse with hot water. Toss linguine with sour cream and margarine. Spoon into a large pasta bowl. Spoon seafood sauce on top. Garnish with lemon wedges and fresh parsley. Serve.

YIELD   6 SERVINGS

LINGUINE WITH RED CLAM SAUCE

PASTA EARNED ITS POPULARITY BECAUSE OF DISHES SUCH AS THIS!

8 oz.	linguine pasta	250 g
10 oz.	can of baby clams	284 mL
2 tbsp.	butter	30 mL
2	garlic cloves, minced	2
2	green onions, chopped	2
½ cup	chili sauce	125 mL
1 tbsp.	lemon juice	15 mL
5½ oz.	can tomato paste	156 mL
1 tbsp.	chopped fresh parsley	15 mL
1 tsp.	salt	5 mL
½ tsp.	pepper	2 mL

- In a large pot, cook linguine according to package directions.
- Meanwhile, drain clams. Reserve liquid.
- In a skillet, heat butter and sauté clams, garlic and onions for 2 minutes.
- Add reserved clam juice, chili sauce, lemon juice and tomato paste. Stir well. Bring to a boil, reduce heat and simmer for 8 minutes. Add parsley, salt and pepper.
- Serve linguine topped with clam sauce.

YIELD   *4 SERVINGS*

SEAFOOD LASAGNE

THE FRUITS OF THE SEA ADD A NEW TWIST TO A FAVORITE DISH

½ cup	margarine	125 mL
3	garlic cloves, crushed	3
½ cup	flour	125 mL
½ tsp.	salt	2 mL
2 cups	milk	500 mL
2 cups	chicken broth	500 mL
8 oz.	mozzarella cheese, grated	250 g
½ cup	chopped green onion	125 mL
1 tsp.	dried crushed sweet basil	5 mL
¼ tsp.	pepper	1 mL
9-12	uncooked lasagne noodles	9-12
2 cups	creamed cottage cheese	500 mL
½ lb.	cooked crab meat OR crab-flavored pollock	250 g
½ lb.	cooked small shrimp	250 g
½ cup	grated Parmesan cheese	125 mL

- In a large saucepan over low heat, melt margarine. Add garlic. Slowly stir in flour and salt, until bubbly and thickened. Remove from heat.
- Add milk and broth. Return to heat stirring constantly until mixture boils. Boil for 1 minute. Remove from heat.
- Add mozzarella cheese, onion, basil and pepper. Stir until cheese melts.
- In an ungreased 9 x 13" (23 x 33 cm) pan spread ¼ of the cheese sauce. Cover sauce with 3-4 noodles. Spread cottage cheese over noodles.
- Cover with ¼ of the cheese sauce. Layer with 3-4 more noodles.
- Cut crab into bite-sized pieces. Spread crab and shrimp over noodles. Cover with ¼ of the cheese sauce. Layer with 3-4 more noodles.
- Spread remaining cheese sauce over noodles. Sprinkle with Parmesan cheese.
- Bake at 325°F (160°C) for 1 hour, or until noodles are tender. Remove from oven. Let stand for 10 minutes before cutting to serve.

NOTE Precooking in boiling water is not necessary with either regular lasagne noodles or oven-ready lasagne noodles.

YIELD *8-9 SERVINGS*

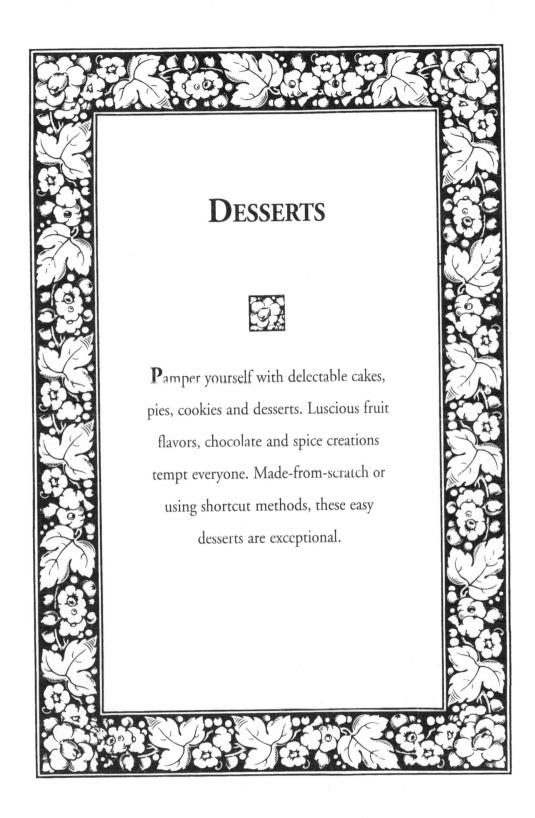

DESSERTS

Pamper yourself with delectable cakes,
pies, cookies and desserts. Luscious fruit
flavors, chocolate and spice creations
tempt everyone. Made-from-scratch or
using shortcut methods, these easy
desserts are exceptional.

PEARS IN BROWN SUGAR SAUCE

WHAT AN ELEGANT CONCLUSION TO A FINE DINNER!

BROWN SUGAR SAUCE:

¼ cup	butter	60 mL
⅔ cup	brown sugar	150 mL
1 tsp.	cinnamon	5 mL
½ tsp.	nutmeg	2 mL
½ tsp.	ginger	2 mL
12	canned pear halves, drained	12
1 qt.	vanilla ice cream	1 L

- In a large skillet, combine the butter, brown sugar and spices. Melt together slowly over low heat. Add the pear halves.
- Simmer slowly, gently turning pear halves over in the sauce.
- To serve, place a scoop of ice cream into individual dessert bowls. Top each with a pear half and some sauce.

VARIATIONS Substitute fresh or canned peaches, apricots or nectarines for pears.

YIELD *8-12 SERVINGS*

PAVLOVA

THIS CLASSIC AUSTRALIAN DESSERT WILL BE A HIT WITH FAMILY AND GUESTS

MERINGUE:

4	egg whites	4
1 cup	sugar	250 mL
1 tbsp.	cornstarch	15 mL
1 tsp.	lemon juice	5 mL

FILLING:

1 cup	whipping cream	250 mL
1 tbsp.	icing sugar	15 mL
	fresh fruit	

- In a mixing bowl, beat egg whites until soft peaks form. Gradually add sugar while continuing to beat. Beat until stiff peaks form.
- Fold in cornstarch and lemon juice.
- Cover a 10" (25 cm) round oven tray with foil. Grease and lightly flour foil.
- Spread ⅓ of the egg whites over the foil-lined tray. With the remaining meringue, spread or pipe a thick border around the meringue base to form a shell.
- Bake at 300°F (150°C) for 1 hour. Turn off oven. Open oven door slightly. Leave meringue shell in oven to cool.
- If meringue shell is made in advance, it should be stored in an airtight container.
- To prepare Pavlova for serving, whip cream and icing sugar together until firm peaks form. Fill meringue shell. Cut fresh fruit and arrange on top of the filling.

YIELD   *8-10 SERVINGS*

CITRUS POPPYSEED CHEESECAKE

FLAVORS THAT BRING THE BEST OUT OF ONE ANOTHER DO IT AGAIN IN THIS
INCREDIBLY SATISFYING DESSERT

ALMOND CRUMB CRUST:

¾ cup	graham wafer crumbs	175 mL
¾ cup	ground almonds	175 mL
1 tbsp.	sugar	15 mL
¼ cup	margarine, melted	60 mL

ORANGE POPPYSEED FILLING:

16 oz.	light cream cheese	500 g
1 cup	sugar	250 mL
4	eggs	4
1 tbsp.	grated orange rind	15 mL
3 tbsp.	flour	45 mL
¼ cup	orange juice	60 mL
¾ cup	whipping cream	175 mL
2 tbsp.	poppy seeds	30 mL

CITRUS GLAZE:

2	eggs	2
¾ cup	sugar	175 mL
2 tsp.	grated orange rind	10 mL
2 tsp.	grated lemon rind	10 mL
¼ cup	lemon juice	60 mL
2 tbsp.	orange juice	30 mL
2 tbsp.	butter	30 mL

- To make the crust, combine all crust ingredients. Press crumbs into the bottom and 1" (2.5 cm) up the sides of a 9" (23 cm) springform pan.
- Bake at 350°F (180°C) for 8 minutes. Cool.
- To make the filling, in a large mixing bowl, beat cream cheese and sugar until smooth. Add eggs, 1 at a time, and continue to beat just until blended.
- Add remaining filling ingredients. Beat until blended. Pour filling into cooled crust.
- Bake at 450°F (230°C) for 10 minutes. Reduce heat to 250°F (120°C) and bake for an additional 40 minutes, or until the center is just set.

Citrus poppyseed cheesecake
(Continued)

- Remove cake from oven. Run a knife around the rim of the pan to prevent cheesecake from cracking. Cool thoroughly at room temperature.
- To make the glaze, in a small saucepan whisk eggs until foamy.
- Add sugar, rind, juices and butter. Cook over low heat, stirring constantly, until smooth and thickened. Cool.
- Spread glaze evenly over cheesecake before serving.

YIELD   ***10-12 SERVINGS***

See photograph on page 157.

Mini cheesecakes
EASY TO MAKE, EASY TO SERVE AND EASY TO EAT

24	vanilla wafers	24
16 oz.	cream cheese	500 g
4	eggs	4
⅔ cup	sugar	150 mL
1 cup	sour cream	250 mL
2 tbsp.	sugar	30 mL
1 tsp.	vanilla	5 mL
	pie filling OR fresh fruit	

- Place a vanilla wafer in the bottom of medium-sized paper cups placed in a muffin tin.
- In a mixing bowl, beat the cream cheese, eggs and sugar until light and fluffy. Spoon over wafers until cups are ⅔ full. Bake at 325°F (160°C) for 20 minutes, or until set. Cool for 15 minutes.
- Meanwhile, in a mixing bowl, combine the sour cream, sugar and vanilla. Beat well. Top each cupcake with 1 tbsp. (15 mL) of this mixture. Return to the oven and bake for an additional 10 minutes. Cool.
- Serve topped with prepared pie filling or fresh fruit.

VARIATION   For cheesecakes with a chocolate crust, use chocolate wafers instead of vanilla wafers.

YIELD   ***24 MINI CHEESECAKES***

See photograph on page 191.

BANANA CHEESECAKE

A FAVORITE CHOICE OF CHEESECAKE FANS

1½ cups	rolled oats	375 mL
½ cup	finely chopped pecans	125 mL
½ cup	brown sugar	125 mL
⅓ cup	melted butter	75 mL
16 oz.	cream cheese	500 g
1 cup	mashed bananas	250 mL
½ cup	sugar	125 mL
1 tbsp.	lemon juice	15 mL
4	eggs	4
1 cup	sour cream	250 mL
3 tbsp.	sugar	45 mL
1 tsp.	vanilla	5 mL
	bananas, for garnish	

- Combine rolled oats, pecans, sugar and butter. Press firmly into the bottom and up the sides of a 9" (23 cm) springform pan. Bake at 350°F (180°C) for 18 minutes, or until golden brown.
- In a mixing bowl, beat together the cream cheese, bananas, sugar and lemon juice. Add eggs, 1 at a time, while continuing to beat after each addition. Pour into crust. Bake at 350°F (180°C) for 35 minutes. While filling is baking, prepare topping.
- Combine sour cream, sugar and vanilla. Spread over hot filling. Return to oven and continue baking for an additional 10 minutes. Cool. Remove from pan. Chill until ready to serve.
- To serve, decorate with freshly sliced bananas.

NOTE   Brush banana slices for garnish with lemon juice to prevent them turning dark, if you are not serving the cake immediately after garnishing.

YIELD   **10-12 SERVINGS**

BANANA SPLIT CHEESECAKE

IRRESISTIBLE!

BASE:

| 2 cups | graham wafer crumbs | 500 mL |
| ½ cup | margarine, melted | 125 mL |

CREAM CHEESE LAYER:

1 cup	butter, softened	250 mL
8 oz.	cream cheese, softened	250 g
1½ cups	icing sugar	375 mL
1 tsp.	almond extract	5 mL

FRUIT LAYER:

| 4 | bananas | 4 |
| 19 oz. | can crushed pineapple, drained | 540 mL |

TOPPING:

| 2 cups | whipping cream, whipped graham wafer crumbs/nuts | 500 mL |

- Combine the graham wafer crumbs and margarine. Press into a 9 x 13" (23 x 33 cm) pan. Bake at 350°F (180°C) for 10 minutes. Cool.
- In a mixing bowl, combine butter, cream cheese, icing sugar and almond extract. Beat until smooth. Spread over cooled base. Refrigerate until firm.
- Slice bananas lengthwise. Layer bananas over cream cheese mixture. Spread crushed pineapple over bananas.
- Top with whipped cream. Garnish with wafer crumbs or nuts. Refrigerate until ready to serve.

YIELD   *12-15 SERVINGS*

FRUIT FLAN

A FOUR SEASON FAVORITE THAT CAN BE UNIQUE IN TASTE AND APPEARANCE
EACH TIME IT IS MADE

2	eggs	2
½ cup	sugar	125 mL
3 tbsp.	oil	45 mL
2 tbsp.	water	30 mL
½ cup	flour	125 mL
1 tsp.	baking powder	5 mL
	strawberries, kiwis, peaches, grapes, blueberries OR other fresh OR drained canned fruit	
	fruit glaze, see method	
	whipping cream, whipped	

- In a mixing bowl, combine eggs, sugar, oil, water, flour and baking powder in the order given. The mixture should be the consistency of pancake batter.
- Pour batter into a well-greased and floured 11" (28 cm) flan pan.
- Bake at 325°F (160°C) for 20 minutes, or until golden. Let cool for 5 minutes. Carefully invert and remove from pan. Chill.
- Arrange fresh fruit in flan. Glaze with a purchased glaze, or melted clear fruit jelly.
- To serve, top with a dollop of whipped cream.

NOTE   The flan base freezes well so it is convenient to always have one frozen on hand as the finishing touches only require a few minutes.

YIELD   ***10-12 SERVINGS***

See photograph on page 157.

FRUIT PIZZA

SERVE THIS POPULAR DESSERT ON HOT SUMMER DAYS WHEN FRESH BERRIES ARE
AT THEIR PRIME!

CRUST:

2 cups	flour	500 mL
½ cup	brown sugar	125 mL
¼ cup	icing sugar	60 mL
1 cup	butter, softened	250 mL

TOPPING:

8 oz.	cream cheese	250 g
½ cup	sugar	125 mL
1 tsp.	vanilla	5 mL
2-3 cups	sliced OR chopped fresh fruit (strawberries, kiwi, oranges, raspberries, etc.)	500-750 mL

GLAZE:

2 tbsp.	cornstarch	30 mL
1 cup	pineapple OR orange juice	250 mL
½ cup	sugar	125 mL
1 tbsp.	lemon juice	15 mL

- In a bowl, combine crust ingredients. Press into a 12" (30 cm) pizza pan. Bake at 350°F (180°C) for 12 minutes, or until golden brown. Cool.
- In a mixing bowl, cream together cream cheese, sugar and vanilla. Spread evenly over cooled crust.
- Arrange fruit in an interesting pattern over the cream cheese mixture.
- In a saucepan, combine the glaze ingredients. Cook slowly and stir until mixture thickens. Pour over fruit. Chill.

VARIATION A 20 oz. (567 g) package of commercially prepared cookie dough could be substituted for the above crust. With floured hands, press the cookie dough evenly over a lightly greased 12" (30 cm) pizza pan and prepare as above.

YIELD *12 SERVINGS*

MARSHMALLOW RASPBERRY SWIRL

ADDS A FESTIVE TOUCH FOR VALENTINE ENTERTAINING

CRUST:

1¼ cups	graham wafer crumbs	300 mL
1 tbsp.	sugar	15 mL
¼ cup	melted butter	60 mL

RASPBERRY FILLING:

3 oz.	raspberry gelatin	85 g
35	large marshmallows	35
½ cup	milk	125 mL
2 cups	whipped topping	500 mL
15 oz.	pkg. frozen whole raspberries, thawed and drained	425 mL

whipped cream
raspberries for garnish

- In a mixing bowl, combine wafer crumbs, sugar and butter. Press evenly into a greased 9" (23 cm) springform pan.
- Prepare the gelatin according to package directions. Chill until partially set.
- In a saucepan over low heat, melt the marshmallows in the milk. Stir to blend well. Let cool.
- In a large bowl, fold the cooled marshmallow mixture into the whipped topping.
- Fold the raspberries into the partially set gelatin.
- Fold the raspberry-gelatin mixture into the whipped topping mixture to get a marbled effect.
- Pour filling into crumb crust. Chill for a few hours before serving.
- To serve, garnish with whipped cream and whole raspberries.

VARIATIONS   This dessert is equally good with other flavors of gelatin and fruit such as peaches, strawberries or oranges.

YIELD   *12 SERVINGS*

GRASSHOPPER PIE

MAKE IN ADVANCE AND SERVE ON A WARM DAY

1⅓ cups	chocolate sandwich cream cookie crumbs	325 mL
3 tbsp.	margarine, melted	45 mL
24	large marshmallows	24
½ cup	milk	125 mL
1½ oz.	envelope, dessert topping mix	42 g
2 tbsp.	crême de menthe liqueur	30 mL
1 tbsp.	crême de cacao liqueur	15 mL
	green food coloring	
	chocolate-flavored flakes OR chocolate cookie crumbs for garnish	

- Combine cookie crumbs and margarine. Press into a 9" (23 cm) pie plate. Chill.
- Combine marshmallows and milk over medium heat until marshmallows melt. Cool until thickened.
- Prepare topping mix as directed on package.
- Fold marshmallow mixture and liqueurs into topping.
- Add a few drops of food coloring to obtain a light, pleasant green color. Fold into marshmallow mixture.
- Spoon filling into chilled crust.
- Garnish.
- Freeze overnight.
- Remove pie from freezer 15 minutes before serving.

YIELD   **8-10 SERVINGS**

PINEAPPLE ALOHA PIE

DELIGHTFULLY SMOOTH AND RICH

1	8" (20 cm) baked graham wafer pie crust, chilled, see below	1
4 oz.	cream cheese	115 g
¼ cup	sugar	60 mL
10 oz.	can crushed pineapple, drained	284 mL
½ cup	whipping cream, whipped sliced fresh fruit for garnish	125 mL

- Prepare the pie crust. Bake at 350°F (160°C) for 10 minutes. Chill.
- In a large mixing bowl, beat the cream cheese until fluffy. Add the sugar and continue to beat. Add the pineapple and mix well.
- Fold the whipped cream into the pineapple mixture.
- Spoon the pineapple mixture into the pie crust. Refrigerate until well chilled.
- To serve, garnish with fresh fruit.

YIELD　　*5 SERVINGS*

GINGERSNAP PIE CRUST

AN EXCELLENT CRUST FOR PUMPKIN FILLING

1⅔ cups	gingersnap crumbs	400 mL
¼ cup	melted butter	60 mL
¼ cup	sugar	60 mL

- In a bowl, combine all ingredients. Press into a 9" (23 cm) pie plate.
- If to be used unbaked, chill thoroughly.
- If to be baked with filling, follow directions for baking filling.

VARIATION　　To make a Graham Wafer Pie Crust, substitute graham wafer crumbs for gingersnap crumbs. To make a Chocolate or Vanilla Crumb Crust, substitute chocolate or vanilla wafer crumbs.

YIELD　　*9" (23 CM) CRUST*

DESSERT

Fruit Flan, page 152
Citrus Poppyseed Cheesecake, page 148

COCONUT CREAM PIE

A BAKED VERSION WHICH IS A DELIGHT TO PREPARE AND SERVE!

1	9" (23 cm) unbaked pie shell*	1
⅓ cup	sugar	75 mL
¼ cup	flour	60 mL
2	eggs	2
1 cup	milk	250 mL
½ tsp.	vanilla	2 mL
1 tbsp.	butter, melted	15 mL
1 cup	finely shredded coconut	250 mL

- In a small bowl, combine sugar and flour.
- In a mixing bowl, beat eggs. Add the sugar mixture and continue to beat until creamy.
- Gently blend in the milk, vanilla and butter.
- Add the coconut. Mix well.
- Pour coconut mixture into pie shell.
- Bake at 350°F (180°C) for 30 minutes, or until the center of the pie is firm.

* Use the pie pastry on page 133 of *Grandma's Touch* or use your favorite pastry recipe.

NOTE	For traditional coconut cream pie, see variation of Banana Cream Pie, page 160.
YIELD	*6 SERVINGS*

BANANA CREAM PIE

THIS TRULY IS A DELICIOUS FLAVOR TREAT FROM YESTERYEAR,
ONE OF GRANDMA'S SPECIALTIES

1	9" (23 cm) baked pie shell*	1
3 tbsp.	flour	45 mL
1 tbsp.	cornstarch	15 mL
½ cup	sugar	125 mL
¼ tsp.	salt	1 mL
2	egg yolks, beaten	2
1 cup	milk	250 mL
1 cup	half and half cream	250 mL
1 tsp.	vanilla	5 mL
2	bananas, sliced	2
1 cup	whipping cream, whipped	250 mL

- In a saucepan, combine flour, cornstarch, sugar and salt.
- Combine egg yolks, milk and cream. Add to dry ingredients. Over low heat, stir and cook until thick. Add vanilla. Cool.
- Place banana slices in pie shell. Pour cooked filling over. When ready to serve, garnish with additional banana slices dipped in lemon juice.
- Top with whipped cream.

* Use the pie pastry on page 133 of *Grandma's Touch* or use your favorite pastry recipe.

VARIATIONS   To make Coconut Cream Pie, coconut may be substituted for bananas. Add ¼ cup (60 mL) shredded coconut to filling. Sprinkle ½ cup (125 mL) shredded coconut on top.

YIELD   *6 SERVINGS*

RHUBARB CUSTARD PIE

UNIQUE AND VERY TASTY

1	9" (23 cm) unbaked pie crust*	1
4 cups	chopped rhubarb	1 L
1 cup	brown sugar	250 mL
2 tbsp.	caramel pudding mix	30 mL
1	egg	1
2	egg yolks	2

MERINGUE:

2	egg whites	2
1 tbsp.	cold water	15 mL
2 tbsp.	sugar	30 mL
1 tsp.	cornstarch	5 mL
½ tsp.	baking powder	2 mL
1 tsp.	vanilla	5 mL

- Prepare the pie shell.
- Place the rhubarb in the pie shell.
- In a small mixing bowl, combine the sugar and pudding mix with 1 whole egg and 2 egg yolks. Pour over the rhubarb.
- Bake at 350°F (180°C) for 1 hour.
- For meringue, in a mixing bowl combine all ingredients. Beat on low speed for 1 minute. Beat at high speed until egg whites stand in peaks. Spread meringue over baked pie. Return to the oven and continue to bake for 10 minutes, or until meringue is lightly browned.

* Use the pie pastry on page 133 of *Grandma's Touch* or use your favorite pastry recipe.

NOTE	Seal meringue to all edges of the pie crust so it won't shrink while cooling.
YIELD	*6 SERVINGS*

STRAWBERRY CUSTARD TARTS

ANOTHER SWEET THAT HAS STOOD THE TEST OF TIME

2 cups	flour	500 mL
2 tbsp.	sugar	30 mL
1 tbsp.	baking powder	15 mL
1 cup	margarine	250 mL
1	egg	1
¼ cup	milk	60 mL
1 tsp.	vanilla	5 mL
1 cup	strawberry jelly	250 mL
2	eggs	2
½ cup	sugar	125 mL
1 cup	coconut	250 mL
1 tbsp.	melted butter	15 mL

- In a mixing bowl, combine the flour, sugar and baking powder. With a pastry blender, cut in the margarine until crumbly.
- In a small bowl, beat the egg and milk together. Add the vanilla. Add the milk mixture to the crumb mixture. Blend well. Refrigerate dough about 1 hour so it is easier to work with.
- Taking small bits of dough at a time, press it into the bottom and up the sides of small cupcake (muffin) tins.
- Place 1 tsp. (5 mL) of jelly in each tart.
- In a mixing bowl, beat the eggs until fluffy. Add the sugar, coconut and melted butter. Mix well. Over the jelly, place about 1 tbsp. (15 mL) of the coconut mixture, or sufficient to fill each tart about ⅔ full.
- Bake at 350°F (180°C) for 20 minutes, or until golden brown.

VARIATIONS Substitute other fruit-flavored jams or jellies for the strawberry jelly. Garnish with sliced fresh fruit if you wish.

YIELD ***ABOUT 2 DOZEN TARTS***

APPLESAUCE SPICE CAKE

WHILE THIS IS BAKING, THE AROMA DRAWS EVERYONE TO THE KITCHEN

2 cups	flour	500 mL
½ tsp.	baking soda	2 mL
1½ tsp.	baking powder	7 mL
14 oz.	can unsweetened applesauce	398 mL
2 tbsp.	cocoa	30 mL
½ tsp.	salt	2 mL
1 tsp.	cinnamon	5 mL
½ tsp.	cloves	2 mL
½ tsp.	nutmeg	2 mL
½ tsp.	allspice	2 mL
2	eggs	2
½ cup	vegetable oil	125 mL
1 cup	sugar	250 mL
¾ cup	raisins	175 mL

- In a large bowl, combine flour, baking soda and baking powder.
- In a separate bowl, combine remaining ingredients. Pour over dry ingredients. Mix well.
- Pour batter into a greased and floured 9 x 13" (23 x 33 cm) baking pan.
- Bake at 350°F (180°C) for 45 minutes, or until cake springs back when lightly touched.
- Frost with Coffee Icing, page 166.

YIELD   *9 X 13" (23 X 33 CM) CAKE.*

TOMATO SOUP SPICE CAKE

MOIST AND SPICY — A MAN'S FAVORITE

2 cups	flour	500 mL
1½ cups	sugar	375 mL
4 tsp.	baking powder	20 mL
1 tsp.	baking soda	5 mL
1½ tsp.	allspice	7 mL
1 tsp.	cinnamon	5 mL
½ tsp.	ground cloves	2 mL
10 oz.	can condensed tomato soup	284 mL
½ cup	soft margarine	125 mL
2	eggs	2
¼ cup	water	60 mL

- In a large mixing bowl, combine the dry ingredients.
- Add the tomato soup and margarine. Beat until well combined.
- Add eggs and water. Mix well.
- Pour batter into a greased and floured 9 x 13" (23 x 33 cm) pan.
- Bake at 350°F (180°C) for 35 minutes, or until cake springs back when lightly touched. Cool.
- Frost with Cream Cheese Frosting, see *Grandma's Touch*, page 149, or with Orange Cream Cheese Frosting, page 166 in this book, or another favorite frosting.

YIELD   *9 X 13" (23 X 33 CM) CAKE*

ORANGE CHIFFON CAKE

SAVE THIS IMPRESSIVE CAKE FOR SPECIAL OCCASIONS

2 cups	sifted cake flour	500 mL
1 tbsp.	baking powder	15 mL
1 cup	sugar	250 mL
1 tsp.	salt	5 mL
½ cup	vegetable oil	125 mL
½ cup	orange juice	125 mL
½ cup	water	125 mL
3 tbsp.	grated orange rind	45 mL
½ tsp.	baking soda	2 mL
7	egg yolks	7
7	egg whites	7
½ tsp.	cream of tartar	2 mL

- In a large mixing bowl, blend together flour, baking powder, sugar and salt.
- In another bowl, mix oil, orange juice, water, orange rind, baking soda and egg yolks. Beat until smooth.
- Form a well in dry ingredients and add orange mixture. Beat until smooth.
- In another large mixing bowl, combine egg whites and cream of tartar. Beat until very stiff peaks form.
- Pour orange mixture over egg whites. Gently fold in (do not stir) orange mixture.
- Pour batter into an ungreased 4" (10 cm) deep tube pan.
- Bake at 325°F (160°C) for 50 minutes, then increase temperature to 350°C (180°C) for 10-15 minutes.
- Turn cake pan upside down on a funnel and cool for 10 minutes. Remove cake from pan. Cool.
- Frost with Orange Cream Cheese Frosting, page 166.

VARIATIONS   To make Poppy Seed Chiffon Cake, substitute ½ cup (125 mL) poppy seeds, soaked in 1 cup (250 mL) water for 2 hours prior to making, for orange juice, water and orange rind.

YIELD   *1 TUBE CAKE*

COFFEE ICING

MOCHA FANS WILL ENJOY THIS ON THEIR FAVORITE CHOCOLATE CAKE

¼ cup	hot water	60 mL
1 tsp.	instant coffee	5 mL
3 tbsp.	butter, softened	45 mL
pinch	salt	pinch
3 cups	icing sugar	750 mL
½ tsp.	rum extract	2 mL

- In a mixing bowl, combine water, coffee, butter and salt. Mix until smooth.
- Add icing sugar. A little more or less may be required to obtain desired consistency.
- Flavor with extract. Mix well.
- Use as a filling or frosting for your favorite cake recipes.

YIELD   *ENOUGH FROSTING FOR A 9 X 13" (23 X 33 CM) CAKE OR 2, 8 X 9" (20 X 23 CM) LAYERS.*

ORANGE CREAM CHEESE FROSTING

8 oz.	cream cheese	250 g
1 tbsp.	orange juice	15 mL
3½ cups	icing sugar	875 mL
pinch	salt	pinch
1 tsp.	grated orange rind	5 mL

- Combine all ingredients. Mix until well blended.
- Use as a filling or frosting for cakes.

YIELD   *ENOUGH FROSTING FOR A CHIFFON OR ANGEL FOOD CAKE, OR FOR A 2 OR 3 LAYER 9" (23 CM) CAKE.*

ALOHA ANGEL DESSERT

A GREAT MAKE-AHEAD FOR A BRIDAL SHOWER OR A PARTY

14 oz.	can crushed pineapple	398 mL
½ tsp.	salt	2 mL
¼ cup	cornstarch	60 mL
½ cup	sugar	125 mL
3	egg yolks, beaten	3
1½ tbsp.	lemon juice	22 mL
3	egg whites	3
½ cup	sugar	125 mL
2 tbsp.	icing sugar	30 mL
1½ cups	whipping cream	375 mL
1½ cups	flaked coconut	375 mL
1	10" (25 cm) baked angel food cake	1

- In a saucepan, combine pineapple, salt, cornstarch and ½ cup (125 mL) sugar. Bring to a boil over medium heat, stirring constantly. Cook until thickened.
- Stir a small amount of thickened pineapple mixture into beaten egg yolks. Stir egg yolk mixture into pineapple mixture. Cook 1 minute longer. Remove from heat. Stir in lemon juice. Cool to room temperature.
- Beat egg whites until foamy. Gradually beat in ½ cup (125 mL) sugar. Continue beating until stiff peaks form.
- Fold cooled pineapple mixture into beaten egg whites.
- In a mixing bowl, combine icing sugar and whipping cream. Whip until stiff. Stir in coconut.
- Fold coconut-whipped cream mixture into pineapple mixture.
- Split angel food cake into 3 layers. Fill and frost with pineapple cream.
- Refrigerate several hours or overnight.

NOTE   Dessert may be frozen if made in advance.

YIELD   *12 SERVINGS*

CHOCOLATE KILLER DESSERT

THIS GET RAVE REVIEWS FOR BOTH PRESENTATION AND TASTE!

19 oz.	chocolate cake mix	510 g
2 tbsp.	Kahlúa liqueur	30 mL
2 x 3 oz.	pkgs. chocolate mousse instant dessert mix	2 x 85 g
1 cup	whipping cream, whipped	250 mL
4	Skor OR Crispy Crunch chocolate bars, crushed	4

- Prepare cake mix according to package directions. Cool.
- Cut half of cake into bite-sized pieces. Freeze remaining half of cake for other occasions.
- In a clear glass trifle dish, place half of the cake pieces.
- Sprinkle with 1 tbsp. (15 mL) of liqueur.
- Prepare mousse dessert mixes according to package directions. Spread half of the prepared mousse over chocolate cake pieces in dish.
- Spread half of the whipped cream on top.
- Sprinkle with half of the chocolate bar crumbs.
- Continue layering with remaining cake pieces, liqueur, mousse, whipped cream and chocolate pieces.
- Chill until ready to serve, at least 3 hours or overnight.

YIELD   12-15 SERVINGS

KAHLÚA CHOCOLATE CAKE

A MUST FOR FANS OF CHOCOLATE

19 oz.	chocolate cake mix	510 g
4 oz.	chocolate instant pudding mix (4-portion size)	113 g
⅓ cup	Kahlúa liqueur	75 mL
¾ cup	oil	175 mL
4	eggs	4
2 cups	sour cream	500 mL
10½ oz.	pkg. chocolate chips	300 g

KAHLÚA CHOCOLATE CAKE
(CONTINUED)

- In a large mixing bowl, combine all ingredients but chocolate chips. Beat well.
- Add chocolate chips and beat again.
- Pour batter into a greased and floured 10" (25 cm) bundt pan.
- Bake at 350°F (180°C) for 50 minutes, or until a toothpick inserted in the center comes out clean.
- Cool on a rack for 10 minutes. Turn out onto a cake plate.
- Frost if desired.

YIELD   *12-15 SERVINGS*

TURTLE CAKE

AN IRRESISTIBLE RICH MOIST PUDDING-LIKE CAKE

19 oz.	chocolate cake mix	510 g
¼ cup	butter	60 mL
1 cup	sweetened condensed milk	250 mL
50	caramel candies	50
1 cup	chocolate chips	250 mL
1 cup	chopped pecans	250 mL
	icing sugar, pecans	

- Prepare cake mix according to package directions.
- Grease and flour a 10" (25 cm) springform pan.
- Pour ½ of prepared batter into springform pan. Bake at 350°F (180°C) for 15 minutes.
- Meanwhile, in a saucepan over low heat, combine butter, condensed milk and caramels until caramels are melted.
- Remove cake from oven. Sprinkle with chocolate chips and pecans. Pour caramel sauce over. Add the remaining cake batter. Bake for an additional 45 minutes, or until a toothpick inserted in the center comes out clean.
- Cool on a wire rack for 10 minutes. Remove from springform pan. Decorate with icing sugar and pecans.

YIELD   *12-15 SERVINGS*

TRIPLE CHOCOLATE CAKE

MORE THAN SATISFYING FOR CHOCOHOLICS!

19 oz.	chocolate cake mix	510 g
6 oz.	chocolate instant pudding mix (6-portion size)	170 g
¼ cup	mayonnaise	60 mL
4	eggs	4
3 tbsp.	almond liqueur	45 mL
1 tsp.	almond extract	5 mL
¾ cup	sour cream	175 mL
½ cup	water	125 mL
½ cup	oil	125 mL
1 cup	chocolate chips	250 mL
½ cup	slivered almonds	125 mL

- In a large mixing bowl, combine all ingredients but chocolate chips and almonds. Beat at medium speed for 2 minutes.
- Add chocolate chips and almonds. Mix well.
- Pour into a greased and floured 10" (25 cm) bundt pan.
- Bake at 350°F (180°C) for 50 minutes, or until a toothpick inserted in the center comes out clean.
- Cool on a rack for 10 minutes. Turn out onto a serving dish.
- Drizzle with Chocolate Butter Icing, see *Grandma's Touch*, page 158.

YIELD   *12-15 SERVINGS*

CHOCOLATE CHERRY REFRIGERATOR CAKE

A TASTY SIMPLIFIED VERSION OF BLACK FOREST CAKE!

3 oz.	pkg. cherry gelatin	85 g
¾ cup	boiling water	175 mL
½ cup	cold water	125 mL
19 oz.	chocolate cake mix	510 g
1½ oz.	env. dessert topping mix	42 g
4 oz.	chocolate instant pudding mix (4-portion size)	113 g
1½ cups	cold milk	375 mL

- Dissolve gelatin in boiling water. Add cold water. Set aside.
- Prepare cake mix and bake in a 9 x 13" (23 x 33 cm) pan according to directions on package. Cool for 20 minutes.
- With a fork, prick holes about 1" (2.5 cm) apart in cake in pan. Pour gelatin mixture over cake. Refrigerate cake.
- In a chilled bowl, blend and whip topping mix, pudding mix and milk until stiff, about 5 minutes. Immediately frost cake. Return to refrigerator until ready to serve.

NOTE   If prepared in advance, frosted cake may be frozen.

YIELD   ***10-12 SERVINGS***

ORANGE RUM CAKE

THE TANTALIZING AROMA OF THIS CAKE IS MATCHED ONLY
BY THE RICH FLAVOR

19 oz.	white cake mix	510 g
4 oz.	vanilla instant pudding mix (4-portion size)	113 g
4	eggs	4
½ cup	cold water	125 mL
½ cup	oil	125 mL
½ cup	rum	125 mL
1 cup	chopped pecans	250 mL
½ cup	brown sugar	125 mL

ORANGE GLAZE:

¼ cup	margarine	60 mL
1 cup	white sugar	250 mL
½ cup	orange juice	125 mL

- In a large mixing bowl, combine cake mix, pudding, eggs, water, oil and rum. Beat well.
- In a small bowl, combine the pecans and brown sugar.
- Grease and flour a 10" (25 cm) angel food or bundt pan.
- Sprinkle half the pecan mixture into the bottom of the pan. Pour in half the cake batter. Sprinkle the remaining pecan mixture over. Pour in the remaining cake batter.
- Bake at 350°F (180°C) for 1 hour.
- Let sit for 10 minutes before turning out onto a serving plate.
- While cake is cooling, prepare Orange Glaze. In a saucepan, melt margarine. Add sugar and orange juice.
- Boil gently for 5 minutes while stirring.
- Prick holes into cooled cake with a skewer. Slowly pour glaze over cake to allow it to soak in.

VARIATION   Substitute orange juice for rum.

YIELD   *16-20 SERVINGS*

PIÑA COLADA DESSERT

A DELICIOUS EVERYDAY DESSERT WHICH TASTES DIVINE

19 oz.	white OR pineapple cake mix	510 g
½ x 12½ oz.	can cream of coconut	½ x 355 mL
14 oz.	can crushed pineapple	398 mL
1 cup	whipping cream, whipped	250 mL
1 cup	coconut, toasted	250 mL

- Prepare cake mix according to package directions. Bake in a greased 9 x 13" (23 x 33 cm) pan or 10" (25 cm) springform pan.
- Prick holes in cake with a fork as soon as it is removed from the oven. Slowly pour the cream of coconut evenly over the cake.
- Spoon undrained crushed pineapple over the cake. Cool.
- Spread whipped cream over cake. Sprinkle with coconut.

NOTE   This dessert is best when made a few hours in advance of serving.

YIELD   **12-15 SERVINGS**

PISTACHIO CAKE

SERVE WITH A SCOOP OF VANILLA OR PISTACHIO ICE CREAM. GREAT!

19 oz.	white cake mix	510 g
4 oz.	pistachio instant pudding mix (4-portion size)	113 g
¾ cup	cold water	175 mL
¾ cup	oil	175 mL
4	eggs	4
1 tsp.	almond flavoring	5 mL

- In a large mixing bowl, combine the cake mix with the pudding mix. Add the water, oil and eggs. Beat for 5 minutes.
- Add the almond flavoring. Beat for another minute.
- Pour batter into a greased 10" (25 cm) bundt or angel food pan.
- Bake at 350°F (180°C) for 50 minutes, or until a toothpick inserted in the center comes out clean.
- Frost or glaze if desired.

NOTE The green color of this cake makes it very appropriate for serving on St. Patrick's Day.

YIELD **12-15 SERVINGS**

ORANGE PINEAPPLE CAKE

A GRANDE FINALÉ TO A YOUNG GIRL'S BIRTHDAY PARTY

19 oz.	lemon cake mix	510 g
½ cup	oil	125 mL
4	eggs	4
10 oz.	can mandarin oranges and juice	284 mL
14 oz.	can crushed pineapple, drained, juice reserved	398 mL
2 cups	whipped topping	500 mL
4 oz.	vanilla instant pudding (4-portion size)	113 g
	orange zest OR segments for garnish	

ORANGE PINEAPPLE CAKE
(CONTINUED)

- In a large mixing bowl, combine the cake mix, oil and eggs. Beat well.
- Add the oranges and reserved pineapple juice. Mix well.
- Pour batter into a greased and floured 12" (30 cm) springform pan.
- Bake at 350°F (180°C) for 35 minutes, or until a toothpick inserted in the center comes out clean. Cool for 10 minutes. Turn out onto a serving dish.
- In a bowl, combine the topping, pineapple and instant pudding. Frost the cake. Decorate with orange zest segments. Chill and serve.

YIELD   *12-15 SERVINGS*

LEMON LOAVES
TASTES JUST LIKE SCRATCH CAKE — BUT EASIER TO MAKE

3 oz.	pkg. lemon gelatin	85 g
1 cup	boiling water	250 mL
4	eggs	4
¾ cup	oil	175 mL
19 oz.	lemon cake mix	510 g

LEMON GLAZE:

½ cup	icing sugar	125 mL
¼ cup	lemon juice	60 mL

- In a small bowl, dissolve gelatin in water. Cool.
- In a large mixing bowl, combine the eggs and oil.
- To the egg mixture, add the cake mix alternately with the gelatin mixture. Beat for 6 minutes.
- Pour batter into 2 greased 5 x 9" (2 L) loaf pans. Bake at 350°F (180°C) for 45 minutes, until a toothpick inserted in the center comes out clean.
- While loaves are baking, mix the glaze ingredients together.
- When loaves are removed from the oven, prick holes in them with a fork, cool for about 5 minutes, then drizzle glaze over warm loaves.

VARIATIONS   Try orange cake mix, gelatin and juice in place of the lemon.
YIELD   *2 LOAVES*

BRANDY BALLS

A TRIED AND TRUE FAVORITE FOR THE HOLIDAY SEASON

2 x 8 oz.	pkg. vanilla wafers	2 x 250 g
½ cup	honey	125 mL
⅓ cup	brandy	75 mL
⅓ cup	white rum	75 mL
1 lb.	walnuts, finely chopped	500 g
	sugar	

- Roll vanilla wafers into fine crumbs.
- In a mixing bowl, combine crumbs, honey, brandy, rum and walnuts.
- Shape into bite-sized balls. Roll in sugar.

NOTE   Make several days in advance as flavor improves with aging.

YIELD   **60 BALLS**

RUM BALLS

THEIR FLAVOR IMPROVES WITH AGE IF YOU CAN KEEP THEM
AROUND LONG ENOUGH

2¼ cups	graham wafer crumbs	560 mL
1 cup	icing sugar	250 mL
¾ cup	finely chopped pecans	175 mL
¼ cup	cocoa	60 mL
⅓ cup	corn syrup	75 mL
¼ cup	rum	60 mL
	chocolate sprinkles, coconut OR chopped nuts	

- In a mixing bowl, combine crumbs, sugar, pecans and cocoa.
- Add the corn syrup and rum. Knead well to blend ingredients.
- Shape into bite-sized balls. Roll in chocolate sprinkles, coconut or nuts.

NOTE   Store in an airtight container for at least a day to permit flavors to blend.

YIELD   **60 BALLS**

FRYING PAN COOKIES

HIGHLY RECOMMENDED BY ALL GRANDMOTHERS

2	eggs, beaten	2
1½ cups	chopped dates	375 mL
¾ cup	sugar	175 mL
1 tsp.	vanilla	5 mL
2 cups	crisp rice cereal	500 mL
1 cup	chopped walnuts OR pecans	250 mL
	flaked coconut	

- In a large skillet, combine eggs, dates, sugar and vanilla. Cook slowly for 10 minutes, or until ingredients are well blended. Cool.
- Add cereal and nuts. Shape into bite-sized balls. Roll in coconut.

YIELD   *APPROXIMATELY 36 BITE-SIZED BALLS.*

AFTER EIGHT TRIANGLES

RESERVED FOR VERY SPECIAL OCCASIONS!

1 cup	margarine	250 mL
8 oz.	milk chocolate	250 g
10 oz.	can sweetened condensed milk	300 mL
1½ cups	seedless raisins	375 mL
14 oz.	digestive cookies, crushed	400 g
14 oz.	pkg. After Eight wafers	400 g
	icing sugar (optional)	

- In a large saucepan, combine margarine, milk chocolate and condensed milk. Melt over low heat. Add raisins.
- Remove saucepan from heat and add cookie crumbs. Stir to blend well. Spread into a greased 10 x 15" (25 x 38 cm) baking or jelly roll pan.
- Spread a layer of After Eight wafers over the batter.
- Refrigerate for an hour, or until firm. Cut into triangles.
- If desired, sprinkle with icing sugar.

YIELD   *96 TRIANGLES*

TOFFEE ALMOND TREATS

A FLAVOR COMBINATION THAT IS HARD TO BEAT

CRUST:

1 cup	flour	250 mL
1 cup	rolled oats	250 mL
1 cup	brown sugar	250 mL
1 tsp.	baking soda	5 mL
½ cup	butter OR margarine	125 mL

TOPPING:

½ cup	corn syrup	125 mL
⅓ cup	brown sugar	75 mL
¼ cup	butter	60 mL
¼ cup	evaporated milk	60 mL
1½ cups	sliced almonds	375 mL
1 tsp.	vanilla	5 mL

- In a mixing bowl, combine flour, rolled oats, sugar, baking soda and butter. Mix until crumbly.
- Press crumbs into a greased 9 x 13" (23 x 33 cm) baking pan. Bake at 350°F (180°C) for 30 minutes.
- In a saucepan, combine the corn syrup, brown sugar, butter and milk. Bring to a boil. Remove from heat. Stir in almonds and vanilla. Spread syrup mixture evenly over crust.
- Bake at 350°F (180°C) for 15-20 minutes.
- When cool cut into triangles.

YIELD   48 TRIANGLES

CARAMEL TOFFEE SQUARES

THESE RATE HIGH ON THE KID'S LIST OF FAVORITES

BASE:

½ cup	butter	125 mL
¼ cup	sugar	60 mL
1½ cups	flour	375 mL

CARAMEL FILLING:

½ cup	brown sugar	125 mL
½ cup	butter	125 mL
2 tbsp.	corn syrup	30 mL
⅔ cup	sweetened condensed milk	150 mL

CHOCOLATE TOPPING:

8 oz.	chocolate chips	250 g
2 tsp.	butter	10 mL

- Combine butter, sugar and flour. Press into a lightly greased 9" (23 cm) square pan. Bake at 350°F (180°C) for 20 minutes. Cool.
- In a saucepan, combine the brown sugar, butter, corn syrup and condensed milk. Bring to a boil. Simmer for 5 minutes, stirring constantly. Pour over the baked base. Cool.
- Over low heat in a saucepan, melt the chocolate chips and butter. Spread over the cooled filling. Chill.
- Cut into squares.

YIELD   36 SQUARES

SEVEN-LAYER SQUARES

THESE FAVORITES ARE ALSO KNOWN AS "HELLO DOLLY" SQUARES

½ cup	melted butter	125 mL
1½ cups	graham wafer crumbs	375 mL
1½ cups	flaked coconut	375 mL
½ cup	chocolate baking chips	125 mL
½ cup	butterscotch baking chips	125 mL
10 oz.	can sweetened condensed milk	300 mL
1 cup	chopped pecans	250 mL

- Pour melted butter into a 9 x 13" (23 x 33 cm) pan.
- Press crumbs into butter.
- Layer the coconut, baking chips, milk and pecans over the crumbs in the order given. Do not mix layers.
- Bake at 350°F (180°C) for 30 minutes.
- As squares cool, loosen edges so milk does not stick to edges of pan.
- Refrigerate until needed. Cut into squares.

YIELD   *24 SQUARES*

OLD-FASHIONED WALNUT SQUARES

THESE NEVER DISAPPOINT THE COOK OR THE TASTERS

1 cup	flour	250 mL
2 tsp.	baking powder	10 mL
1 tbsp.	sugar	15 mL
¼ tsp.	salt	1 mL
½ cup	margarine	125 mL
1	egg	1
1 tsp.	vanilla	5 mL
3 tbsp.	milk	45 mL
1¼ cups	brown sugar	300 mL
2	eggs	2
¼ cup	flour	60 mL
1 tsp.	baking powder	5 mL
½ cup	coconut	125 mL
1 cup	chopped walnuts	250 mL

- In a mixing bowl, combine the flour, baking powder, sugar and salt. With a pastry blender, cut in the margarine.
- In a small bowl, combine the egg, vanilla and milk. Add to the dry ingredients. Pat into an ungreased 9" (23 cm) square pan. Bake at 350°F (180°C) for 10 minutes.
- In a mixing bowl, combine the brown sugar and eggs. Beat until frothy. Add the flour and baking powder. Beat until well blended. Add the coconut and walnuts. Pour over the baked crust.
- Bake at 325°F (160°C) for 45 minutes, or until a knife inserted in the center comes out clean.

YIELD   *36 SQUARES*

LEMON SQUARES

GUARANTEED TO BECOME A FAMILY FAVORITE!

1 cup	rolled oats	250 mL
1 cup	flour	250 mL
½ cup	coconut	125 mL
1 tsp.	baking soda	5 mL
½ cup	brown sugar	125 mL
½ cup	margarine	125 mL
½ cup	lemon juice	125 mL
10 oz.	can sweetened condensed milk	300 mL

- In a large mixing bowl, combine the oats, flour, coconut, baking soda and brown sugar. Add the margarine and mix until crumbly.
- Press half the crumb mixture into a greased 9" (23 cm) square pan.
- Mix the lemon juice with the condensed milk until well blended. Pour over the crumb base. Cover the filling with the remaining crumbs.
- Bake at 350°F (180°C) for 35 minutes, or until golden brown.

YIELD   *30 SQUARES*

APRICOT BARS

A PLEASANT ADDITION TO A TRAY OF FAVORITES

BASE:

½ cup	butter	125 mL
¼ cup	brown sugar	60 mL
1 cup	flour	250 mL

APRICOT TOPPING:

½ cup	flour	125 mL
½ tsp.	baking powder	2 mL
2	eggs	2
¾ cup	brown sugar	175 mL
½ cup	coconut	125 mL
7½ oz.	jar apricot baby food	213 mL

- In a mixing bowl, combine butter, brown sugar and flour until crumbly. Spread in a greased 9" (23 cm) square pan. Bake at 350°F (180°C) for 20 minutes.
- Beat the topping ingredients together until fluffy. Pour over base. Bake at 350°F (180°C) for 30 minutes, or until a knife inserted in the center comes out clean.

NOTE   These bars are not very sweet and they freeze well.

YIELD   **30 BARS**

BACKPACK ENERGY BARS

DON'T LEAVE HOME WITHOUT THESE WHEN GOING HIKING, CYCLING
OR CAMPING!

WHOLE-WHEAT BASE:

⅓ cup	butter	75 mL
¾ cup	brown sugar	175 mL
1	egg	1
¾ cup	whole-wheat flour	175 mL
½ cup	Grapenut cereal	125 mL
½ tsp.	baking powder	2 mL
¼ tsp.	salt	1 mL
⅛ tsp.	baking soda	0.5 mL
1 tsp.	grated orange rind	5 mL

CRUNCHY TOPPING:

3	eggs	3
¼ cup	brown sugar	60 mL
½ cup	Grapenut cereal	125 mL
½ cup	chopped dry apricot halves	125 mL
½ cup	coarsely chopped prunes	125 mL
½ cup	raw sunflower seeds	125 mL
½ cup	slivered almonds	125 mL

- In a large mixing bowl, combine the butter, brown sugar and egg. Beat well. Add the remaining ingredients for the base. Mix well.
- Press base mixture into a greased 9 x 13" (23 x 33 cm) pan.
- In another mixing bowl, beat the 3 eggs. Add the sugar. Mix well. Add the remaining topping ingredients. Combine well. Spread over the base.
- Bake in a 350°F (180°C) oven for 40 minutes, or until a toothpick inserted in the center comes out clean.

VARIATIONS   Any combination of dry fruit or nuts may be substituted for those given.

YIELD   *24 BARS*

BUTTER FINGERS

DELICATE AND DELICIOUS

1 cup	butter	250 mL
1/3 cup	icing sugar	75 mL
2 cups	flour	500 mL
1 cup	chopped pecans OR walnuts	250 mL
	icing sugar OR chocolate	

- In a mixing bowl, combine butter and icing sugar. Gradually work in flour. Stir in chopped nuts.
- Form dough into small cylinders about the size of a little finger.
- Bake on ungreased cookie sheets on the middle rack at 350°F (180°C) for 12-15 minutes.
- When baked, dredge fingers with icing sugar or dip ends into melted chocolate.

YIELD   *3 DOZEN FINGERS*

CHOCOLATE-DIPPED STRAWBERRIES

AN IMPRESSIVE ENDING TO A PARTY WITH SPECIAL FRIENDS

1 qt.	strawberries with stems	1 L
4 oz.	chocolate	125 g
1 tbsp.	paraffin	15 mL

- Wash and dry strawberries leaving the stems on.
- In a small saucepan, melt the chocolate and paraffin. Remove from heat.
- Holding the strawberries by the stem, dip them into the chocolate. Place on a wire rack to set.
- If chocolate becomes too thick, return to low heat only for a short period of time.

YIELD   *VARIES WITH THE SIZE OF THE BERRIES.*

ICEBOX COOKIES

YOU'LL BE GLAD GRANDMA SHARED THIS ONE

1 cup	butter	250 mL
2 cups	brown sugar	500 mL
2	eggs	2
¼ tsp.	almond extract	1 mL
4 cups	flour	1 L
1 tsp.	baking soda	5 mL
1 tsp.	cream of tartar	5 mL
1 cup	chopped nuts, currants OR candied peel and cherries	250 mL

- In a large mixing bowl, cream together butter and sugar. Beat in eggs and extract.
- In another bowl, sift together flour, baking soda and cream of tartar.
- Add nuts or fruit to the dry ingredients. Mix well.
- Add dry ingredients to butter mixture. Stir until well combined.
- Divide dough into 4 parts. Form each part into a roll 1½" (4 cm) in diameter and pat onto waxed paper. Lift, roll and smooth to form even cylinders. Wrap each cylinder well and refrigerate.
- To bake, remove roll from refrigerator. Unwrap the roll and cut into ¼" (6 mm) slices.
- Place dough slices on lightly greased cookie sheets and bake at 350°F (180°C) for 10-12 minutes, or until edges are lightly browned.

YIELD   *8 DOZEN COOKIES*

CRACKER JACK COOKIES

KEEP THIS RECIPE HANDY, THERE WILL BE NUMEROUS REQUESTS FOR IT

1½ cups	flour	375 mL
2 cups	oatmeal	500 mL
2 cups	crisp rice cereal	500 mL
1 cup	coconut	250 mL
1 tsp.	baking soda	5 mL
1 tsp.	baking powder	5 mL
1 cup	margarine, softened	250 mL
1 cup	brown sugar	250 mL
1 cup	white sugar	250 mL
2	eggs	2
2 tsp.	vanilla	10 mL

- In a large bowl, combine the flour, oatmeal, cereal, coconut, baking soda and baking powder.
- In a smaller bowl, combine the margarine and the sugars. Mix until well blended.
- Add the eggs and vanilla to the sugar mixture. Mix well.
- Pour the egg mixture over the dry ingredients. Mix to combine well.
- Drop batter by tablespoons (15 mL portions) onto greased cookie sheets.
- Bake at 350°F (180°C) for 8-10 minutes, or until lightly browned.

YIELD   *6 DOZEN*

CHOCO BANANA PEANUT COOKIES

THREE POPULAR FLAVORS COMBINE FAVORABLY

1 cup	brown sugar	250 mL
¾ cup	peanut butter	175 mL
½ cup	butter	125 mL
¾ cup	mashed bananas	175 mL
2	eggs	2
1 cup	white flour	250 mL
1 cup	whole-wheat flour	250 mL
2 tsp.	baking powder	10 mL
¼ tsp.	salt	1 mL
¾ cup	chocolate chips	175 mL
¾ cup	coarsely chopped unsalted peanuts	175 mL

- In a mixing bowl, beat together the brown sugar, peanut butter and butter. Stir in the bananas and eggs. Blend well.
- In a separate bowl, combine the remaining ingredients. Add to the banana mixture. Mix well.
- Drop batter by tablespoons (15 mL portions) onto an ungreased cookie sheet.
- Bake at 350°F (180°C) for 12-15 minutes. Cool. Store in an airtight container.

YIELD   *4 DOZEN COOKIES*

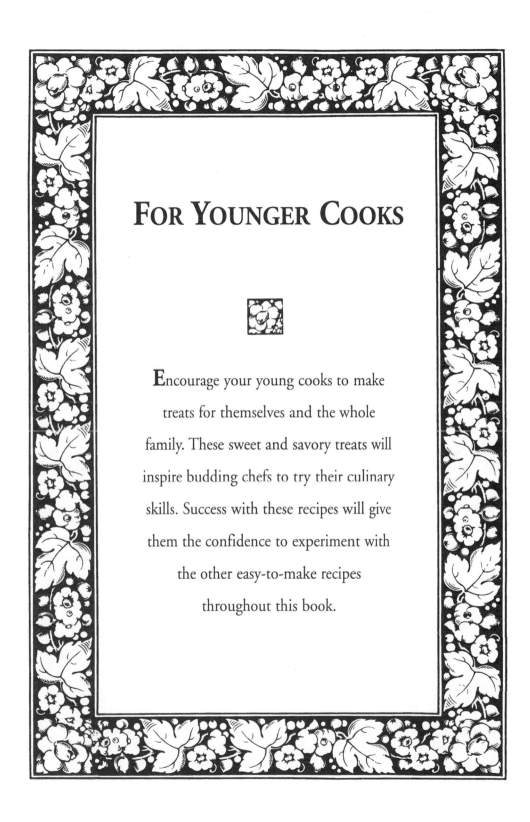

FOR YOUNGER COOKS

Encourage your young cooks to make
treats for themselves and the whole
family. These sweet and savory treats will
inspire budding chefs to try their culinary
skills. Success with these recipes will give
them the confidence to experiment with
the other easy-to-make recipes
throughout this book.

PEANUT BUTTER CONES

THESE DECORATIVE DESSERTS CAN SERVE AS TABLE DECORATIONS
UNTIL DESSERT TIME

⅓ cup	margarine	75 mL
½ cup	peanut butter	125 mL
1 cup	brown sugar	250 mL
2	eggs	2
1 tsp.	vanilla	5 mL
2 cups	flour	500 mL
½ tsp.	salt	2 mL
2½ tsp.	baking powder	12 mL
¾ cup	milk	175 mL
24	flat-bottomed ice cream cones	24
½ cup	jam	125 mL

- In a mixing bowl, cream together margarine and peanut butter. Add sugar. Beat until light and fluffy. Add eggs and vanilla. Beat well.
- In a smaller bowl, combine the flour, salt and baking powder. Add alternately to creamed mixture with milk.
- Fill cones half full with batter. Place 1 tsp. (5 mL) of jam on top of batter. Then fill cones with the remaining batter.
- Place cones in muffin tins. Bake at 350°F (180°C) for 25 minutes. Cool.
- Decorate as desired.

NOTE   These are great for children to decorate either for a birthday or a special holiday. Smarties, peanut halves, raisins, jellybeans and small gumdrops are favorite decorations.

YIELD   *24 CONES*

FOR YOUNGER COOKS

"Dirt" Dessert, page 196
Mini Cheesecakes, page 149

Snackin' Crackers

CHILDREN AND ADULTS LOVE THIS FLAVORFUL AND CRUNCHY SNACK.
CHILDREN ENJOY COMBINING AND MIXING THE INGREDIENTS
FOR THIS FAMILY TREAT

6 cups	Shreddies cereal	1.5 L
6 cups	bite-sized Cheddar cheese fish crackers	1.5 L
1 cup	vegetable oil	250 mL
1 tbsp.	melted butter	15 mL
1 oz.	pkg. dry ranch salad dressing mix	28 g
1 tsp.	dried dillweed	5 mL
1 tsp.	lemon pepper	5 mL

- Spread cereal and crackers in a large baking pan.
- In a small bowl, combine remaining ingredients. Pour over cereal and crackers. Stir to mix.
- Bake at 325°F (160°C) for 1 hour, stirring frequently.

VARIATION   Miniature Ritz Crackers may be used as a substitute for Shreddies.

YIELD   *12 CUPS (3 L)*

CRISPY NIBBLERS

A VERSION OF NUTS 'N' BOLTS WITH LESS SODIUM

4 cups	Cheerios cereal	1 L
4 cups	Shreddies cereal	1 L
4 cups	puffed wheat cereal	1 L
1 cup	sunflower oil	250 mL
2 tsp.	garlic powder	10 mL
2 tsp.	onion powder	10 mL
¼ cup	Worcestershire sauce	60 mL
	peanuts, pretzels (optional)	

- In a large roasting pan, combine all but optional ingredients.
- Bake in a 200°F (100°C) oven for 1½ hours, stirring occasionally.
- Add optional ingredients if desired.

YIELD   *3 QUARTS (3 L)*

PEOPLE CHOW

THIS INTERESTING SNACK FOR YOUNG PEOPLE TASTES
ESPECIALLY GOOD AROUND A CAMPFIRE!

12 oz.	box Crispix cereal	350 g
1 cup	smooth peanut butter	250 mL
¾ cup	chocolate chips	175 mL
¼ cup	melted margarine	60 mL
1½ cups	icing sugar	375 mL

194

PEOPLE CHOW
(CONTINUED)

- Place cereal in a large bowl.
- In a saucepan over low heat, bring peanut butter, chips and margarine almost to the boiling point. Pour over cereal. Let sit a few minutes to cool. With oiled hands, gently mix well.
- Place icing sugar in a paper bag. Add coated cereal. Shake well to coat cereal with sugar.
- Cool. Serve.

NOTE   This freezes well so it can be made in advance of a pajama party or weekend camp out.

YIELD   *12 CUPS (3 L)*

POPCORN BALLS
INVITE YOUR FRIENDS TO SHARE IN THE ENJOYMENT OF MAKING AND EATING THIS TREAT

10 cups	popped popcorn	2.5 L
¼ cup	butter	60 mL
⅓ cup	oil	75 mL
40	large marshmallows	40
1 cup	Smarties (optional)	250 mL
1 cup	baking gumdrops (optional)	250 mL
1½ cups	peanuts (optional)	375 mL

- Place popcorn in a large bowl or baking pan.
- In a saucepan over low heat, combine butter, oil and marshmallows until marshmallows are melted. Pour over popcorn. With oiled hands, mix well. Add optional ingredients as desired.
- Shape the popcorn mixture into balls or press into a buttered 9 x 13" (23 x 33 cm) pan or a 10" (25 cm) bundt or angel food pan.

VARIATIONS   To add flavor and color for a special occasion or holiday, 3 tbsp. (45 mL) of a flavored gelatin can be added to the melted marshmallow mixture before pouring over the popcorn.

YIELD   *20 POPCORN BALLS*

"DIRT" DESSERT

THIS RECIPE IS FUN TO MAKE AND FUN TO EAT

8 oz.	cream cheese	250 g
½ cup	margarine	125 mL
¾ cup	icing sugar	175 mL
4 cups	whipped topping	1 L
6 oz.	pkg. vanilla instant pudding	170 g
2 cups	milk	500 mL
30	chocolate vanilla cream cookies, crushed into fine crumbs	30
10-12	gummy worms	10-12

- In a large bowl, cream together cream cheese, margarine and icing sugar.
- Add whipped topping, instant pudding and milk. Blend until well combined.
- In a 7-8" (18-20 cm) flower pot, layer cookie crumbs ("dirt") alternately with cream cheese mixture, beginning and ending with the crumbs.
- Place gummy worms in the top layer so they are half exposed.
- To decorate, place artificial flowers in the "dirt".

VARIATIONS   Individual servings can be made by layering "dirt" with cheese mixture in small seedling pots, miniature pails or decorated styrofoam cups. Decorate with small plastic flowers and worms. These are a real hit for a child's birthday party.

YIELD   *10-12 SERVINGS*

See photograph on page 191.

SPECIAL K SQUARES

A GREAT SUCCESS AT BAKE SALES

2 cups	Spanish peanuts	500 mL
6 cups	Special K cereal	1.5 L
1 cup	sugar	250 mL
2 tbsp.	butter	30 mL
1 cup	white corn syrup	250 mL
1½ cups	peanut butter	375 mL
1 cup	chocolate chips	250 mL
1 cup	butterscotch chips	250 mL

- Spread peanuts in a 9 x 13" (23 x 33 cm) pan.
- Put cereal into a large mixing bowl.
- In a saucepan, combine sugar, butter and syrup. Bring to a boil. Remove from heat. Add peanut butter. Stir well. Pour over cereal. Mix well.
- Quickly press cereal mixture over peanuts in the pan.
- Melt both flavors of chips together. Spread over cereal mixture. Cool. Cut into squares.

YIELD   *16 SQUARES*

ALMOND ROCA

AN EXCELLENT KITCHEN GIFT FOR THE YOUNG ONES TO MAKE AND TO GIVE!

½ x 14 oz.	pkg. of graham wafers	½ x 400 g
1 cup	butter	250 mL
¾ cup	brown sugar	175 mL
½ cup	sliced almonds	125 mL

- Line a jelly roll pan with aluminum foil. Arrange whole graham wafers in a single layer over the pan.
- In a saucepan, bring the butter and sugar to a boil. Simmer for 5-6 minutes. Pour over the wafers in the pan. Sprinkle with shaved almonds.
- Bake at 350°F (180°C) for 8 minutes. Cool. Break into pieces.

YIELD   *60 PIECES, 6 CUPS (1.5 L)*

EATMORE BARS

A TAKEOFF OF THAT FAMOUS CHOCOLATE BAR— AND EQUALLY ENJOYABLE!

1 cup	chocolate chips	250 mL
1 cup	peanut butter	250 mL
1 cup	corn syrup	250 mL
1 cup	brown sugar	250 mL
3 cups	crisp rice cereal	750 mL
1 cup	unsalted peanuts	250 mL
¼ cup	raw sunflower seeds	60 mL
⅓ cup	sesame seeds (optional)	75 mL

- In a saucepan over low heat, combine and melt the chips, peanut butter, syrup and sugar.
- In a large bowl, combine the remaining ingredients.
- Pour chocolate mixture over cereal, nut mixture. Mix well.
- Spread cereal mixture into a greased 9 x 13" (23 x 33 cm) pan. Chill. Cut into bars.

YIELD   *15 BARS*

OREO COOKIES

19 oz.	chocolate cake mix	510 mL
⅓ cup	oil	75 mL
2	eggs	2

- In a large mixing bowl, combine the above ingredients. The dough will be very stiff.
- With the use of a melon baller or other kitchen gadget, make uniform-sized, about 1 tbsp. (15 mL), balls of dough. Place dough balls on a greased cookie sheet. Pat down with a glass bottom dipped in sugar.
- Bake at 350°F (180°C) for 10-15 minutes, or until done.
- When cookies are cool put together in pairs with a cream cheese icing, see *Grandma's Touch*, page 149.

VARIATIONS   For special occasions such as Hallowe'en use an orange cake mix with chocolate icing as a filling. For St. Patrick's Day use a white cake mix with green-colored filling. Use your imagination. Peanut Butter Cookies can be made the same way using a 19 oz. (510 g) yellow cake mix, 1 cup (250 mL) of peanut butter, ½ cup (125 mL) oil, 2 tbsp. (30 mL) of water and 2 eggs. Fill with peanut butter icing or the filling of your choice.

YIELD   *48, 2½" (6 CM) COOKIES OR 24 SANDWICH CREAM COOKIES*

SLAB COOKIES

GREAT WITH A GLASS OF MILK AFTER SCHOOL

1 cup	margarine	250 mL
1 cup	brown sugar	250 mL
1 tsp.	vanilla extract	5 mL
2 cups	flour	500 mL
1 cup	baking chips, chocolate OR butterscotch	250 mL

- In a mixing bowl, beat together margarine and sugar. Add vanilla. Mix well.
- In another bowl, combine flour and baking chips. Add to creamed mixture. Mix well.
- Pat dough mixture into a greased 10 x 15" (25 x 38 cm) baking or jelly roll pan.
- Bake at 350°F (180°C) for 20 minutes. Cut into squares while warm.

YIELD **30 SQUARES**

---

milk

lemon cheas V.G.

JELLIED YOGURT

A NUTRITIOUS SNACK, AND IN THE FLAVOR OF YOUR CHOICE

3 oz.	pkg. gelatin *jello*	85 g
1 cup	boiling water	250 mL
2 cups	yogurt OR buttermilk	500 mL

used kefir v. G.

- In a mixing bowl, combine gelatin with water. Stir until gelatin is dissolved.
- Add yogurt or buttermilk. Stir. Pour into individual serving dishes. Chill to set before serving.

YIELD **5 SERVINGS**

FINGER JELLIES

THIS FUN SNACK TO EAT WITH THE FINGERS COMES IN VARIOUS
COLORS AND SHAPES

| 4 x 3 oz. | pkg. gelatin | 4 x 85 g |
| 2½ cups | boiling water | 625 mL |

- In a mixing bowl, dissolve gelatin powder in water. Mix well.
- Pour into a 9 x 13" (23 x 33 cm) pan.
- Chill until firm.
- To unmold, dip pan in warm water for 15 seconds. Cut jelly into squares or cut out figures with cookie cutters. Remove squares or figures from pan to a plate. Refrigerate.

VARIATION   Depending on the occasion or season, make 2 or 3 colors or shapes to decorate a party table.

PLAYDOUGH

MAKE A FEW BATCHES OF VARIOUS COLORS AND CREATE!

1 cup	flour	250 mL
2 tsp.	cream of tartar	10 mL
½ cup	salt	125 mL
1 cup	boiling water	250 mL
2 tbsp.	vegetable oil	30 mL
	food coloring	

- In a saucepan, combine all ingredients except food coloring.
- Add a few drops of food coloring and stir in until desired color is obtained. Mix well.
- Stir over low heat until of playdough consistency. Remove from heat.
- When not being used, store in the refrigerator in an airtight container.

OOBLECK

THIS IS A VERY MOIST AND FLEXIBLE FORM OF PLAYDOUGH, MORE LIKE "SLIME", SO, OF COURSE, CHILDREN LOVE IT!

2	parts water	2
1	part cornstarch	1
	food coloring of your choice	

- Combine cornstarch, water and food coloring. Store in a covered container or wrap in plastic wrap.
- If making a large batch, divide the oobleck in several portions and color each portion a different color.

NOTE This dries out very quickly if it is not well wrapped.

INDEX

INDEX

INDEX

INDEX

Share GRANDMA TODAY with a friend

Please send _____ copies of *GRANDMA TODAY* or *GRANDMA'S TOUCH* at $16.95 per book, plus $4.00 (total order) for postage and handling:

GRANDMA'S TOUCH _____ x $16.95	$ _____
GRANDMA TODAY _____ x $16.95	$ _____
Handling Charge_____	$ __4.00__
Subtotal_____	$ _____
In Canada add 7% G.S.T. _____ (subtotal x .07) =	$ _____
Total enclosed _____	$ _____

U.S. or International orders payable in U.S. funds.

NAME: _____

STREET: _____

CITY: _____ PROV.STATE: _____

COUNTRY: _____ POSTAL CODE/ZIP: _____

A Great Gift Idea

Please make cheque or money order payable to: Averine Enterprises Ltd.
116 Langholm Drive
St. Albert, Alberta
T8N 4M4

For fund-raising or volume purchases, contact AVERINE ENTERPRISES LTD. for volume rates. Please allow 3-4 weeks for delivery.

Price is subject to change.

Share GRANDMA TODAY with a friend

Please send _____ copies of *GRANDMA TODAY* or *GRANDMA'S TOUCH* at $16.95 per book, plus $4.00 (total order) for postage and handling:

GRANDMA'S TOUCH _____ x $16.95	$ _____
GRANDMA TODAY _____ x $16.95	$ _____
Handling Charge_____	$ __4.00__
Subtotal_____	$ _____
In Canada add 7% G.S.T. _____ (subtotal x .07) =	$ _____
Total enclosed _____	$ _____

U.S. or International orders payable in U.S. funds.

NAME: _____

STREET: _____

CITY: _____ PROV.STATE: _____

COUNTRY: _____ POSTAL CODE/ZIP: _____

A Great Gift Idea

Please make cheque or money order payable to: Averine Enterprises Ltd.
116 Langholm Drive
St. Albert, Alberta
T8N 4M4

For fund-raising or volume purchases, contact AVERINE ENTERPRISES LTD. for volume rates. Please allow 3-4 weeks for delivery.

Price is subject to change.

GRANDMA'S TOUCH

— Tasty, Traditional and Tempting

by

Irene Hrechuk and Verna Zasada

Now you can enjoy your special childhood favorites as Grandma used to make them, updated for today's busy, health-conscious cooks. Enjoy your favorite comfort food from your British, Chinese, French, German, Italian, Irish, Mexican, Russian, Scandinavian and Ukranian grandmothers. These recipes, using readily available ingredients, are intended for beginner and experienced cooks. First printing sold out in only 6 months!

Retail $16.95   7" x 10"
208 pages   10 colored photographs

GRANDMA'S TOUCH

— Tasty, Traditional and Tempting

by

Irene Hrechuk and Verna Zasada

Now you can enjoy your special childhood favorites as Grandma used to make them, updated for today's busy, health-conscious cooks. Enjoy your favorite comfort food from your British, Chinese, French, German, Italian, Irish, Mexican, Russian, Scandinavian and Ukranian grandmothers. These recipes, using readily available ingredients, are intended for beginner and experienced cooks. First printing sold out in only 6 months!

Retail $16.95   7" x 10"
208 pages   10 colored photographs